The 4 P's of Marriage™

Personal, Private, Public & Permanent

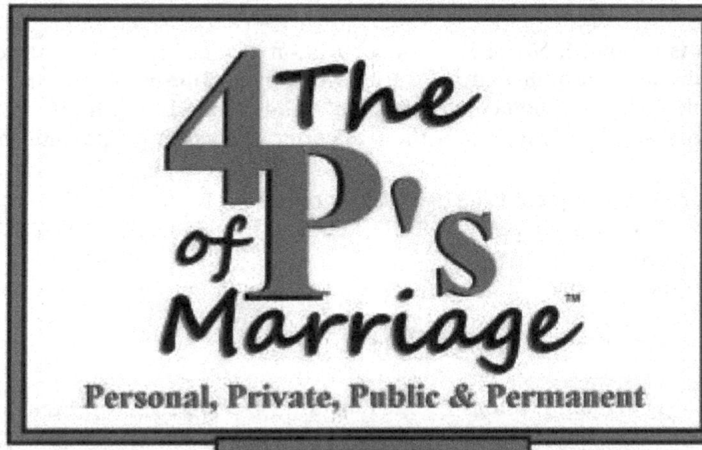

PRECIOUS D. GRAHAM

DONALD E. GRAHAM JR.

THE 4P'S OF MARRIAGE

Published by Promise & Destiny Group Inc.
Lansdale, PA. 19446
www.promisedestinygroup@gmail.com

Printed in the United States of America 2016 – First Edition
Book Cover Design by Donald E. Graham Jr.
Back Cover photo © DSQ Photography

Library of Congress Cataloging-in-Publications Data
The 4P's of Marriage/Precious D. Graham, Donald E. Graham Jr.
p.cm.
Includes bibliographical references and scriptural references.

ISBN 978-1533255440 (pbk.)

1. Graham, Precious D. 2. Graham Jr., Donald E. 3. Inspirational 4. Christianity 5. Religion 6. Encouragement

153325544X

Unless otherwise indicated, all Scripture quotations are taken from the Holy Bible.

Verses marked KJV are taken from the King James Version of the Bible.

Table of Contents

In Loving Memory of

Leonard Gist, Don Thomas & Stafford Bailey

"What therefore God hath joined together,
let not man put asunder." - Mark 10:9

Preface

God places an elevated value on the institution and covenant of marriage. Marriage is a spiritual union, and it is both holy and honorable. (Hebrews 13:4) Human beings must be committed to the covenant union and not just to the person they marry. Yes, there is a considerable difference between the two.

When married couples are only committed to each other, deterioration is right around the corner. We convey that because of how we as human beings waver from one path to another. As a result we easily vacillate through our lack of equilibrium.

Remaining steadfast and unmovable means you don't opt for the quickest reason to divorce when things don't go your way or when your spouse becomes difficult or unlovable at times. Storms and shifts will occur in the marriage and some days you as a couple may feel as though you are on a never ending roller coaster ride.

Thanks be to God for His presence and for being a refuge in times of trouble. It is when we lose our faith in marriage that we allow the enemy to enter. We have learned over the years in order to keep our marriage fresh we needed to refresh at times and seek out others to look at their beginning faith, persistent faith, trusting faith, confirming faith and witnessing faith, in order to share with each while learning from others.

Therefore, permanency in marriage is an ongoing process of steps. God is the author and finisher of His word and this fact also applies to marriage. God is the originator and creator of marriage, and He has provided the blueprint for you and your spouse to have faith in until death due you apart. God's word in and of itself is a legal document. When faith seems weak and storms arise, you are always on safe ground when you hold on to God's scriptures of faith. Therefore find the scriptures that promise those things that you pray for in your marriage. Consider the following…

"Love is patient, love is kind, and is not jealous: love does not brag and is not arrogant, does not act unbecomingly: it does not seek its own, is not provoked, does not take into account a wrong suffered, does not rejoice in unrighteousness, but rejoices with the truth: bears all things, believes all things, hopes all things, endures all things. Love never fails: but if there are gifts of prophecy, they will be done away; if there are tongues, they will cease; if there is knowledge, it will be done away." (1 Cor 13:4-8)

Since we know that God cannot fail, there should never be a *faith failure* in your marriage. You can always find comfort, joy and peace in God's word even in the midst of the trials and tribulations of your marriage. Always remember that God made a promise that you can have whatsoever you ask for if you keep His word in your heart and on your mind. Whenever you feel like giving up and it seems as if there is no hope or faith, maintain

God's word in your heart as it will reinforce the journey of a godly marriage.

The 4 P's of Marriage Workshop is designed to help couples prepare for a God honoring and personally satisfying marriage. We found this class to be very beneficial, as it provided couples with Christ-centered, spirit-filled, Bible-based instructions for building a healthy, joyful, and permanent marriage.

Our resonation of *The 4P's of Marriage* came by listening and applying the word of God to our lives, which has enabled us to witness and partake in the godly marriage that He promised. If God did it for us, we know beyond a shadow of a doubt that He can do it for you. Keep the faith!

Submitted by:
Joyce & Chaplain William Taylor III, Ph.D.

Introduction

It was in the Fall of 2014 when we had an interesting discussion about what we felt were the principles of marriage. At the time we found ourselves ministering to numerous couples who were experiencing hardships in their marriage. Along with the some of the obvious advice we were able to provide from a spiritual perspective (fasting, praying, reading the bible etc.) we also realized that there was a need for practical application that couples could use as a foundation to build upon. Both of us recalled learning about Strategic Marketing during our respective undergraduate studies, and one concept in particular that stood out was the Marketing Mix. The Marketing Mix is a business tool used in marketing and by marketers. The marketing mix is often crucial when determining a product or brand's offer, and is often associated with the four P's: *Product, Price, Place,* and *Promotion*.

As we considered the need for providing couples with some basic essentials for navigating married life, we came up with our own marketing mix for marriages (if you will) called the Four P's of Marriage. The Four P's describes how marriage is *Personal, Private, Public*, and *Permanent*. Over the next few months we created a syllabus for a marital enrichment workshop based on the same name, and God opened up an opportunity for us to teach a seven week workshop in the Spring of 2015 at our church. The purpose of the *4P's of Marriage* is to provide couples with practical application and tools needed to enrich their marriage. We reinforce biblical principles of marriage during our class, while providing each couple with an opportunity to share their thoughts, concerns, and frustrations in a safe environment.

We believe that God can use each of us to help the other deal with "blind spots" that are often overlooked. We all have areas in our lives in which we need to grow or bad habits we need to overcome. Sometimes these things are easy for our spouse to see, but difficult for us to see in ourselves. If we keep a teachable spirit, God can use our spouse to help us grow to be a better person, a better spouse, and more like Christ.

This is more difficult than it sounds. Human nature tends to be defensive and stubborn. When our spouse tries to help us see a weak area, we tend to react by just pointing out one of his or her weaknesses while excusing our own! Of course, it is especially difficult for us to be pliable when our spouse does not communicate a teachable spirit of his or her own. Yet, if we are determined to keep a genuine teachable spirit, our marriages can soar to new heights.

Good marriages don't just happen by chance. A good marriage takes energy, intentional effort and commitment. The key to a good marriage is to regularly and purposefully invest the good things that will help your marriage grow into a deep, rich and fulfilling relationship. Think of your marriage like a bank account of sorts. The more you invest into it the more there is available for you to enjoy. If little is invested, you can't expect to draw much from it. The purpose of this book is to help you and your spouse understand why your marriage is *personal, private, public and permanent*. Furthermore, it is our prayer that as you read this book, that you will be biblically encouraged and spiritually strengthened in your marriage relationship. We thank you in advance for following us as we lead you on this wonderful journey!

Donald & Precious Graham

"Marriage is personal to us because we think it has affected us most in the areas of our personhood. As individuals, we are better. Even before we got married, it was not something either of us felt pressured into. It was a personal decision based upon listening to God and not moving in our own perceived strength or mindsets. Learning to lean on God for every decision can be difficult; learning to trust God in spite of what you see or don't see in a relationship really grows you up as individuals. Marriage creates an area for personal growth that hardly anything else can replicate."

- *Candace and Hakiem Wilkins*

What is a Christian Marriage?

A Christian marriage is one where a man and a woman decide to make a covenant commitment with one another, and to God, by serving Him together. Needless to say there are many professing Christians who are married, but the real question that begs to be asked is, *"Are they serving the Lord together?"* A Christian marriage is one that should be entered into for the purpose of bringing glory and honor to God. Marriage is a sacred union that should never be entered into impulsively or taken lightly. A man and a woman should give careful consideration during the engagement period, before vows are exchanged, to ensure both parties are making an informed decision.

God's intention for marriage is that once a man and a woman are united in holy matrimony, they must remain married until death with the following exception. Jesus said that the only reason for divorce is adultery (Matthew 5:32). When He was asked about

Moses giving permission for a man to divorce his wife, Jesus said this was allowed due to the "*hardness of heart*" of the men. He went on to explain that when a man and a woman are united in marriage they are to act as though they are one person. He concluded by saying, *"Therefore what God has joined together, let not man separate"* (Mark 10:9).

Of course we know that there are many people, including Christians, who get married for a variety of other reasons. They marry because their friends are getting married. They marry for lust, security, wealth, fame, children, and sometimes they even see marriage as a means of emancipation from their parents. Some mistakenly think they are getting married because they "love" the other person. The most important reason that a man and a woman are to marry is to bring glory to God (1 Corinthians 10:31).

Before marriage, the couple is to consider whether or not they are compatible and if they are choosing to get married for the right reasons. Premarital counseling is a vital part of this process. This is where both parties can discuss one another's insecurities, fears, pet peeves, and personality traits that could otherwise become problematic in the future.

A Christian Wife

The Bible says in Proverbs 18:22 that, "*He that finds a wife, finds a good thing and obtains favor from the Lord.*" A woman who desires to be married must first recognize her value. She must believe beyond a shadow of a doubt that she is indeed a "good thing" because that is what her future husband is hard-wired to find. A great wife and partner in marriage. The problem is that he often doesn't have a clue of what that looks like, and many times, his wife is not too sure herself! Needless to say, a Christian wife is one that is trustworthy. Every husband desires a wife that he can place his total trust in. Your husband wants to know that you will always support him even when it looks like he is failing. He gets confidence out of the fact that you will not give up on him when times become difficult. His trust in your ability to stand with him is very important.

A Christian wife must take care of herself, *and then her husband*. We may have just lost some of you with that statement, but please consider our explanation. Sisters, how can you even begin to care for anyone else if you constantly neglect yourself? Furthermore, do not assume that you know what your husband needs. One of your highest priorities is to partner with your husband to ensure that his needs are met. Since your husband is the only one that can effectively communicate what those needs are, as his wife, *you are empowered to define the parameters*.

A Christian wife is also creative and resourceful. A husband, who is not insecure, actually enjoys celebrating his wife's ability to do something special. It could be her ability to cook, teach, sing, plan and coordinate events, etc. He wants to make a big deal about your gifts and talents. Why not showcase them to your husband? Be creative in your relationship with your husband. Be resourceful and find ways to make things work even during difficult economic seasons.

A Christian wife must understand and agree with the biblical teaching that the man she is to marry will be the head of the household (Genesis 3.16; 1 Corinthians 11.3; 1 Peter 3.6), and that marriage is not a 50-50 proposition. She must be learn how to submit to him in all things (Ephesians 5.22-24) gladly, joyfully and respectfully. We will discuss that dreaded topic of *submission* more fully in a later chapter! In marriage, we must subdue our own egos and selfish pride for the sake of the family. The excitement and romantic feelings of a new relationship fade in time, and the husband and wife will begin to see and resent each other's faults. That is when an authentic "Christian Love" (kindness, respect, benevolence) must take over. True Christian love is not about feelings and emotions; but it is something we must make the effort to practice every day.

A Christian Husband

A Christian husband must understand and agree with the biblical teaching that he is to love and care for his wife as Jesus loves and cares for His wife, the church (Ephesians 5.25). He must be willing to die to himself daily to care for his wife. He must put her needs before his own. A Christian husband, who loves and cares for his wife, is one who desires to meet all of her physical needs, such as housing, healthy food, clothing and medical care. (Exodus 21.10) He is equally concerned with meeting her mental needs (conversation), emotional needs (expressing his love for her verbally and in deeds) and spiritual needs (praying with her and leading the family in worship).

It is also imperative that a husband give honor his wife (1 Peter 3.7). Honoring one's wife means a husband is to never criticize, mock, make fun of, ridicule, belittle, scream, demean, or humiliate her in public or private. A husband must treat his wife as if she were more important than himself: *"Do nothing according to contention or vain glory, but in humility esteem one another above yourselves. Consider not the things of yourselves, but also the things of each other."* (Philippians 2.3-4). Most couples that desire to marry "feel" they are in love with each other. The very last thing any man or woman should ever consider first when planning to marry is only their "feelings" of love. Our feelings are almost always questionable, if not flat out wrong. Why? It is because our hearts (inner man) are deceitful above all things and incurable (Jeremiah 17.9). That is why we can never trust only our feelings and emotions. If we could, there would not be so many divorces once all those euphoric feelings fade away and only the true personality and the marriage partner emerges.

Two people must be equally yoked so they can do the work of the Lord together. If they are not, all biblical principles of marriage fall into chaos. An unbelieving husband cannot ask his wife to do as he asks when he is not led by the Lord and has no spiritual discernment. It is important to understand God's teachings in the Bible so we do not fall into godless marriages, which only lead in suffering. *"Do not be unequally yoked together with unbelievers. For what fellowship has righteousness with lawlessness? And what communion has light with darkness? And what accord has Christ with Belial? Or what part has a believer with an unbeliever?"* (2 Corinthians 6:14-15)

A Realistic View of Marriage

We have to stop asking of marriage what God never designed for it to be…perfect happiness, conflict-free living, or a 24/7 never-ending supply of rainbows and butterflies. We must learn to appreciate what God designed marriage to provide: partnership, spiritual intimacy and ability to pursue Him collectively as husband and wife. We have found that the most common misconception Christians have about marriage is that they will ultimately find their *soul-mate*, or someone who will complete them 100%. However, the problem with looking to another human to complete you is that you end up placing unrealistic expectations upon them. We are to find our fulfillment and purpose in God . . . and if we expect our spouse to be 'God' to us, he or she will fail every day. No person can live up to such lofty expectations.

We all have bad days, disagree with our spouse, and at times behave selfishly. In spite of these imperfections, God created the husband and wife to steer each other in His direction. For example: *When a wife forgives her husband and shows compassion, he learns how to receive God's forgiveness and acceptance as well. In that moment, his wife is actually modeling God to him, revealing God's mercy to him, and helping him to see with his own eyes the love of Christ at work in their marriage.*

While it is easy to understand why God would create a selfless union for a self-centered world, it is far from easy trying to live it out on a daily basis. So before the household bills pile up, and before communication breaks down and you're just plain irritated with your husband or wife, we would like to offer these reminders to help ease the tension:

God created marriage as a loyal partnership between a man and a woman. Marriage is the fundamental foundation for building a family. God designed sexual expression for married couples to procreate and cultivate intimacy. Marriage is a reflection of God's covenant relationship with His people. We see this parallel throughout the Bible. For instance, Jesus refers to Himself as the "bridegroom" and to the kingdom of heaven as a "wedding banquet." These points demonstrate that God's purposes for marriage extend far beyond personal happiness. Let us be perfectly clear that God isn't *against* happiness per se, but marriage promotes even higher values and standards. God did not create marriage just to give us a pleasant means of repopulating the earth and raise our children, but He established it as an illustration of the relationship between Christ and the church.

To marry as God intends men and women to marry is to illustrate this most sublime of relationships—the relationship of the Lord Jesus Christ to those who believe on him, and the relationship of the church to Jesus, to the one who loved us and who gave himself for us. God established marriage so that a Christian husband and a Christian wife could act out in their own relationship the relationship that Christ has to you and me and thereby point men to Him as the supreme love, bridegroom, husband, protector, and provider of his church. Once you are able to embrace this truth, you will be well on your way to having a blessed and happy marriage. For you will have the spiritual motivation and overall orientation to make a happy marriage possible.

Learning How to Serve Your Spouse

He spends the entire evening at the office again. She spends money without entering it in the checkbook. He hangs out with his buddies instead of spending time with the kids. From irritating habits to weighty issues that seem impossible to resolve, loving your spouse through the tough times isn't easy. But the same struggles that drive us apart also shed light on what we value in marriage. One thing we try to make clear to the couples we counsel, is that "finding happiness" should not be the ultimate goal of marriage. If you live long enough you will find that happiness is based upon *what happens*. It is inevitable that if happiness is your primary goal, you will be contemplating divorce as soon as the happiness begins to subside. If receiving love is your primary goal, you might be tempted to dump your spouse as soon as they start being less attentive and lovable. But if you marry for the glory of God, to model His love to your spouse and your children, and to reveal His witness to the world, then divorce should never be a consideration.

Couples who've survived a potentially marriage-ending situation, such as infidelity or a life-threatening disease, may continue to battle years of built-up resentment, anger or bitterness. So, what are some ways to strengthen a floundering relationship — or even encourage a healthy one? Here are some practical tips:

- Focus on your spouse's strengths rather than their weaknesses.
- Encourage rather than criticize.
- Pray for your spouse instead of gossiping about them.
- Learn and live what Christ teaches about relating to and loving others.

Young couples in particular can benefit from this advice. After all, many newlyweds aren't adequately prepared to make the transition from seeing one another several times a week to suddenly sharing *everything*. More than likely, annoying habits and less-than-appealing behaviors will surface. Yet as Christians, we are called to respect everyone…including our spouse.

Mission & Vision Statement

For those of you who work in Corporate America, the title of this chapter is not foreign, as you already understand the language and pathology that surrounds having a mission and vision statement.

For those of you who are not as familiar, we can pretty much summarize a mission and vision statement as the standard and critical elements of a company's organizational strategy. Most established companies develop organizational mission statements and vision statements, which serve as foundational guides in the establishment of company objectives. The company then develops strategic and tactical plans for objectives.

During our 4P's of Marriage Workshop, we came up with the idea to have each couple to come up with their very own mission and vision statement. We thought it would be a great idea if they were to collectively develop short term and long term goals that would chart a course for success for their marriage.

Your mission statement for your marriage will be the affirmation of the fundamental purpose and focus of your marriage. An effective mission statement will (1) serve as a filter to separate what is important from what is not, (2) clearly state who will be served and how, and (3) communicate a sense of intended direction to the entire marriage. Think of the mission as something to be accomplished and the vision a something to be pursued for that accomplishment.

A *Marriage Mission Statement* helps us to focus on how we want our marriage to bear fruit. Even when day-to-day living is mundane or difficult, this mission statement will keep your eyes focused on a greater prize. It is usually much shorter than your Marriage Vision Statement, as its purpose state the overall mission and goal of your marriage.

Here are two keys to making a Marriage Mission Statement:

1. **Identify your overall mission.** Ask, "*What kind of spouse does God uniquely call me to be within the context of my marriage?*"
   For example: "*I feel God uniquely calls me to support my spouse's gifts and career drive by being flexible about my own work for a season. This allows us to keep our marriage in balance while the kids are still at home.*"
2. **Break the overall mission down to manageable components.** Ask, "*What can we do within the next two months to get closer to the big goal? What steps can we take within the next six months?*"

In a nutshell, love and marriage requires work. You have to be willing to work to create the type of marriage you want every single day. It is an on-going journey. A marriage mission statement provides a valuable road map. It essentially allows you to begin your journey with the end in mind.

In the same way, a successful *Marriage Vision Statement* allows you and your partner to dream, to imagine the life that you would like to live together, and to determine the course of your relationship. It is like drawing a map that you will use on the journey that you are taking toward building a vibrant, healthy connection. Your Marriage Vision Statement not only helps you and your spouse chart a path for success for your marriage, but it also sets the trajectory for both of you to work toward. Renowned motivational speaker, Les Brown says, *"People don't fail because they aim too high and miss. They often fail because they aim too low and hit!"* So ask yourself…what are you aiming for in your marriage?

The Marriage Vision Statement should be aligned with each of your strengths and core values, and it should reflect the important aspects of each of your lives. A vision statement for your marriage should be an aspirational description of what you both would like the marriage to accomplish. It is intended to aid as a guide for selecting existing and future courses of action. If you feel stuck or are worried that your vision may not match your partner's, bear in mind that you are creating a map of new possibilities to help guide you, not a statement of exactly how things will be.

Your visions are not carved in stone; they will change as you and your partner change and grow, which explains why it is often much longer than your Marriage Mission Statement. Its purpose is to strengthen the teamwork between you and your spouse as you take the necessary steps toward building your life together.

To create your Marriage Vision Statement, you should begin by answering the following questions:

Your Marriage

- How do you want to spend time together?
- When do you want to spend time together?
- What problem areas do you want to overcome?
- In what areas do you want your relationship to grow?

Your Family

- What are your hopes and dreams for your family and children?
- How do you aspire to be with your own parents or your siblings?

Your Friends

- What kinds of friendships do you value?
- How much time do you feel is important to spend with friends?
- Which friends do you share in common?

Your Finances

- What are your thoughts about the way you earn a living?
- How do you think about savings?
- How do you envision financing your children's college education or your retirement?
- Do any of your dreams need to be included in your financial plans?

Your Spiritual Walk

- How do you define your spirituality?
- Is belonging to a religious group important to you?
- Do you need to agree on educating your children about spirituality or religion?

Your Community

- How do you define community?
- Is it important to you to be part of a larger community?
- How do you want to create community? (neighbors, organizations, religious groups etc.)

Too often, people get stuck when they think about creating a vision, especially if their relationship feels hopeless and overwhelming. They worry that their vision may not be important or might be too different from their partners. It is not uncommon to feel anxious or guilty for wanting something in your life when you have been used to denying yourself.

Take your time and create your vision and mission statements over several days (or weeks) if necessary. Just remember you can't get to your destination without a map! While it would be ideal to create a vision statement with your partner, you can also do it on your own and invite your partner to listen to the dreams that you have for yourself and your relationship. Find a quiet time when the two of you will be free from distractions to share your vision.

Don't be afraid to spend time tweaking and praying about your mission statement. It is important that you and your spouse be in full agreement with the final version. Adjust the wording into clear and concise language that both of you can understand. Reread it daily for about 2 weeks. If you want to commit them to memory, we suggest that you post your mission and vision statements in a prominent place in your home. Ask God to help you and your spouse to live them out. To further assist you, we have provided our mission and vision statements below, just in case you and your spouse would like to use them as a guide during the process of creating your own.

Graham's Marriage Mission Statement

"Our marriage will help others fulfill God's promise so they can walk into their destiny."

Graham's Marriage Vision Statement

"As spouse, parent, and minister, we will seek divine aid to enable us to show the love of God first to each other, and then the world. We will use our powers to create a safe space to grow, learn, and share. And by the guidance of the Holy Spirit use our gifts and talents to bring marriages far from God; raised and restored to a life centered in Christ."

Submitting in Love

Submission: From a Woman's Perspective

The topic of submission is a touchy subject that many women don't like to talk about, don't like to teach about, and often times don't even want to hear about! It is sometimes viewed as a sign weakness, and rarely as a sign of strength. It is a concept that goes against the grain of our human nature. Unfortunately, many have taken one of the most wonderful aspects of marriage and made it seem appalling. They have taken something that is Holy and made it horrible, something that is right and made it seem wrong. Our assumptions and lack of biblical knowledge about submission leaves many of embattling instead of embracing.

However, we are here to dispel those misguided assumptions and perceptions. Most married women remember this word being brought up numerous times as they prepared to walk down the aisle many years ago. A lot of women believe that in order to be submissive you should have a gentle and quiet spirit. But what if gentle and quiet are two words that you never associate with yourself? It is enough to give even the most assertive woman pause, as they wonder if they will ever be willing or able to fulfill the perfect submissive role they keep hearing about. *Ah, yes... submission!* We all see the need for it and it is something that we are all called to do. Man, woman, child young or old, married or single.

We are instructed to submit:

- to God (James 4:7),
- to governmental authority (Romans 13:1-7),
- to the church or religious authority (Hebrews 13:17),
- wives/husbands (Ephesians 5:22-24 and Col 3:18),
- children/parents (Ephesians 6:1 and Col 3:20),
- slaves/masters (employees/employers, 1Peter 2:18),
- younger/older (1Peter 5:5), and
- to one another in love (Ephesians 5:21, 1Peter 5:5).

But before we talk about what submission is, let's be clear about what it is not. Submission is not about being used, submission is not silence, and submission is not passivity. Being submissive does not mean you are weak, feebleminded or a constant pushover. Submission in and of itself is not a bad word. In Ephesians 5:22-33, the apostle Paul speaks a three-fold message that is directed at wives. They are to *submit to*, be *subject to*, and to give *reverence to*.

In contrast, the apostle points out time and again the importance of a husband *loving his wife*. So in essence, Paul is saying that there is reciprocity involved in this relationship. A wife can only submit to a husband who not only loves her, but who demonstrates that love towards her. Isn't it interesting how we tend to focus only on the *submission* piece, which is merely only part of the story? *So why do many wives struggle with verse 22 in the text? Why do they cringe every time they read this verse that implores them to submit or be submissive to their husband?* It is important for us to obtain a proper understanding of the word *submission.* This is so important because the meaning of the word "submit" has to be clearly understood or else many problems can *and will* continue to arise.

The American Heritage Dictionary defines "submit" as "to yield or surrender (oneself) to the will or authority of another" now the English word *submit* comes from a Latin root which means "to let down, reduce, or yield." Picture yourself kneeling before someone. Even our modern language hints at its roots: to have ***a*** "***sub***-*mission*" The prefix sub means to be; **1.** situated under or beneath: subterranean **2.** Secondary in rank; subordinate:

So when we talk about submitting or submission, it means that the mission is secondary, situated beneath and yields to a greater one. Now the New Testament Greek word is *hupotasso*, which means "to put under or arrange under." It is a military word that refers to lower-ranking soldiers arranging themselves under the orders of higher officers.

Embracing this concept also helps us to understand that submission comes from an acknowledgment of the proper *order* and *authority*. Now is it starting to make sense? You see, in order to submit in love or have someone submit to you in love we must understand that submission is not something that is forced upon another person. When someone submits themselves, they are doing so freely and willingly. Once you begin to peel back the layers of what society says submission is, it won't be long before its true meaning is revealed. Let's look at this a little bit closer.

Submission is Voluntary

You can attempt to force anybody to do what you want them to do. You can threaten them with your words if they don't do what YOU WANT them to do, you can beat them until you do what YOU want them to do. You can withhold something from them until they do what YOU WANT them to do. But true submission is an attitude of the heart that cannot be forced, coerced, or dictated.

You can force someone to submit, but if there is resentment and bitterness in their hearts, they are not ***in*** submission. Parents know that children can be made to obey out of fear of punishment, but true submission is when someone lovingly yields to your instructions not your demands and not your threats...When you loving lead, guide and instruct me and I loving yield you it...that is a totally different thing and that is submission.

When we talk about the submission of the wife to her husband I would first ask, what mission you are arranging yourself under. When we talk about the submission of a wife to a husband he must first submit to the ultimate authority. When we talk about the submission of the wife to her husband it must be an attitude that she voluntarily chooses.

Men who have tried to use this verse to force their wives into submission have never succeeded. Sure, some have intimidated or condemned their wives into some measure of compliance, but that's not the submission Paul was teaching about here. Notice that Paul instructed the wives to submit, rather than instructing the husbands to *make* their wives submit. Submission is a choice, not a punishment. How can a husband demand or force his wife into submission when God does not even do so. James 4:7 says Submit yourselves, then, to God. Resist the devil, and he will flee from you. We know that all authority comes from God; the chain of authority is not the question. We know that the full order of authority is God — Christ — Man — Woman.

We know that all things are from God, through God, and to God, so He is the highest authority. Jesus Himself recognized God's authority and was submissive to it. I can and moreover want to submit to what is patient, and kind and not envious, and does not boast, it is not proud. It is not rude, and is not self-seeking. I can and I want to submit to what is not easily angered, and keeps no record of wrongs. And does not delight in evil but rejoices with the truth. I can and I want to submit to what always protects, always trusts, always hopes, and always perseveres.

Submission: From a Man's Perspective

We believe that one of the main reasons why many people struggle with the word "submission" is because they neglect to apply it within the context of love. Let us turn our attention to the husbands about that word submission. A husband must realize that the word submission is not one-sided. It is not just designated or relegated to his wife, but both of them are called to submit.

When you look at Ephesians 5:21 it says, *"Submit one to another out of reverence for Christ."* Why do we submit ourselves to Christ? Because He loved us first and He assumes the role of a husband when He identifies with us. That is why the apostle Paul tells us in verse 25, *"Husbands love your wives as Christ loved the church and gave himself up for her."* It all comes back to that word LOVE. Yes L-O-V-E….Love. We're going to keep saying it until you get tired of it!

Husbands must understand that:

- **Love is** the key that opens up the door to your wife's heart.
- **Love is** what allows you to view your wife and your marriage within the proper perspective.
- **Love is** what causes you to look her fault and see her needs.
- **Love is** what allows a husband to apply 1 Peter 3:7 to his marriage. This is where the apostle Paul says: *"Likewise ye husbands, dwell with them (meaning your wives) according to knowledge. Giving honor unto the wife as unto the weaker vessel, and as being heirs together of the grace of life, that your prayers may not be hindered."*

That is the kind of *love* that we all should have in a marriage. But you know what? Before we even begin to operate in that kind of *love*, we must first have a clear understanding of what the word *love* is. Now the bible says in all thy getting, get an understanding. So let's dig a little deeper. What is love? What is the meaning of love? Well let's take a look at Webster's Dictionary where we will find the actual definition.

Love is defined as…

: strong affection for another arising out of kinship or personal ties <and they provide the example of a maternal love that a mother has for her child>

: attraction based on sexual desire : affection and tenderness felt by lovers *(3)*: or it can be an affection based on admiration, benevolence, or common interests.

However, we know that love is not just an emotion. For if *love* were just an emotion, then God would not have commanded us to love. But *love* is something we do. The Bible says in 1 John 3:18, *"My little children, let us not love in word, neither in tongue; but in deed and in truth."*

In the Greek there are three different types of love: ***Eros***, ***Philia*** and ***Agape***.
Eros *is where we get the word erotic, and it has its root in sensuality, passion and sexual love for another person.*
Philia *refers to brotherly love; as in a close fellowship or relationship. This is where the city of Philadelphia took its surname.*
Then there's **Agape** *Love. It is considered the most powerful, the most noteworthy and the most trustworthy. That is because it is an unconditional act of the sheer will.*

So essentially, what this means is that *love* is not only an action word, but it is a call to action. What do we mean by that? Well you can't just tell someone you *love* them with lip service while you display actions that are contradictory of the very words you are speaking. Jesus eluded to this hypocrisy in the gospel of Matthew 15:8, *"These people honor me with their lips but their hearts are far from me."* So if Jesus is able to make a comparative analysis between our words and our actions, it is not a stretch to believe that your spouse is able to do the same thing.

In fact, you can stand outside on the corner with a bullhorn and yell at the top of your lungs how much you *love* your wife. You can serenade her with her favorite *love* song or whisper sweet nothings in her ear. Yet *none* of those things will matter if you are not expressing your *love* for her through the actions that you display on a daily basis. If you need to know what that type of love looks like. Well you don't have to look any further than 1 Corinthians 13:4-7;

"Love is patient, love is kind. It does not envy, it does not boast, it is not proud. It does not dishonor others, it is not self-seeking. It is not easily angered, it keeps no record of wrongs. Love does not delight in evil but rejoices with the truth. It always protects, always trusts, always hopes, always perseveres."

In closing, we now see that from a husband's perspective, submission is directly tied to the love that he has for both God and his wife. A husband who is secure in himself should have no problem at all submitting his love, his respect, his affection, his material possessions, and protective covering to his wife. It is not a form of weakness on his part, but rather, an intentionally display of vulnerability and transparency before her. At the end of the day, both husbands and wives should stop viewing *submission* as a dirty word, and start viewing it as a word that is able to clean up the dirty areas in us called *pride, ego, arrogance,* and *selfishness*.

Would You Marry You?

Some time ago, we posed this question to a friend of ours during a conversation about relationships that have gone awry. During the conversation, in her plunge toward self-pity, this individual began to lament about the state of her personal affairs, citing one futile relationship after another. *"I don't know what else to do."* With exasperation she cynically sneered, *"Just when I think I've found someone 'special' and things are going well, he ends up leaving me." How does this happen that I pick the same men who cheat on me time after time?"*

That's when we asked her to humor us since we knew we were about to ask her a question that might strike her as a bit weird. Would you marry you? *"You're right that is a weird question. Well no, I wouldn't want to marry anyone like me!"* She went on to state that she was amazed that anyone liked her at all.

That response or a variation of its kind often followed when we posed that same question to other people. Our ability to look inward at our own proclivities and shortcomings will go a long way toward building the healthy relationships we desire; not just in romantic expression but in all the personal interactions of our lives.

While our tendency might be to bury or dismiss those parts of ourselves that we don't want to acknowledge, this deep seated inner truth will only serve to undermine any positive changes and inner strength we strive toward. Initially our tendency might be to assess what our partners bring to the proverbial party without assessing what we have to offer. Are we that emotionally available person we are seeking? Do we remain open to constructive criticism and risk being known or do we defend ourselves into isolation staunchly committed to defending our self-righteous deception? Are we refusing to identify our own self-inflicted wounds and negative attitudes that may be keeping us from having a fruitful, loving relationship with people who genuinely want to love us?

These are the hard difficult conversations and essential questions that need to be answered. Only when we like the person we are and work toward becoming 'our best self' will we attract that very same energy which we seek in others. That first step begins by defining what we want to change about ourselves and being honest about who we are.

If you don't really know what it is you want to change about yourself because you are too close for honest introspection, start with observing behavior in others that we find uncomfortable or unpleasant. These behaviors that we observe in others act as our reflective internal barometer. In essence by being willing to note these unlikable behaviors in others we are facing reflections of our true selves and that is a good indication that we are ignoring who we truly are. For example, are you the type of woman who is very critical of others, especially the men in your life? Do you take the time to carefully consider your response when you are angry, or do you just shoot from the hip, with no regard to whom your words might impact? If your answer to these questions is yes, then ask yourself if you would you be willing to marry a man who possessed those same qualities.

In contrast, are you the type of man who is jealous and insecure? Do you make selfish financial decisions that end up negatively impacting your family's future? Do you spend all day on Sunday watching football while neglecting the needs of your wife, your children, and your home? If your answer to these questions is yes, then ask yourself if you would you be willing to marry a woman who possessed those same qualities.

The initial work in defining what we want to change takes an honest assessment of our most rejected parts of ourselves. It is easier to seek the completion of ourselves and acquire what we believe we inherently lack than to actually empower it from within. How often are we drawn to attractive people while believing deep down that we ourselves are not as good looking or unattractive?

When we accept and love our qualities without seeking to acquire them, we form the strongest foundation for authentic, loving relationships. By beginning with that one simple but profound step, we begin the enlightened journey toward feeling inner peace, joy, and fulfillment. As propositions go, there is absolutely no better partner with whom you can say, "I do!"

Section One Questions

1. **What does the term *"Christian Marriage"* mean to you?**

2. **Describe the ways in which you submit to your husband?**

3. **Describe the ways in which you love and honor your wife.**

4. **Would you marry someone like you? Why?**

Notes

"Marriage is private to us because of our covenant commitment with one another. The covenant is a confidentiality agreement between us and God that, if broken, will cause strife and tribulation. We made a covenant with God and each other which is fundamental and uniquely us. God is the only One that sees everything, the brokenness and beauty of our lives together and He is the One that restores and rejoices in the marriage with us. It is okay to have an accountability couple with years and experience who are objective and who will remind you to keep God in the center. However, your accountability couple should not just provide you with their insight and opinions, but they should also remind you about your covenant to God and one another, and to pray earnestly before the Lord. But, ultimately, we are accountable to-and-for one another because we are one flesh."

- *Victoria & Raymond Monts*

Everything is not for Everybody

The subject of disclosing marital problems to your friends is one that should be treaded upon lightly. As ministers, we often hear individual stories from a spouse about how their marriage is in trouble. Sometimes the first impression we feel when hearing this confidential piece of information, is that the individual is being a bit disloyal to their spouse by telling us their marital woes. However, it is important to add that people often share their marital problems, not in a spirit of complaint, but in a manner of regret and with the air of someone who feels like they need to unburden themselves to a trusted friend.

It is more than likely that their spouse wouldn't be too happy about them sharing that their marriage was far from perfect, yet we can also put ourselves in their shoes. If we were them we would want to talk to someone if we believed our marriage was in trouble. This brings us to the question of, *"Who should you share your marital problems with?"* One of the most important things to consider when it comes to sharing anything about your marriage, is trust.

Trust is often the barometer by which we measure our friendships and it should be the litmus test for providing the intimate details of your union. Think about it, if you know someone is a gossiper, then why on earth would you trust them with your personal information? The way that you hear them handle the details of someone else's life should give you a pretty good indication as to how they would handle your information.

Another problem with sharing details about your marriage with other people, is that they may not always look at things objectively. This is especially true when it comes to family members. The people in your family (parents, siblings, aunts, uncles, and cousins, etc.) are often too close to the situation to offer a clear, concise, and fair evaluation of the situation. All they know is that you are their blood and at the end of the day, it will always be thicker than water. It is inevitable for a mother to sympathize with her son as he laments over the misgivings of his wife, and vice-versa when it comes to a father and his daughter.

This puts the other spouse in a precarious position, because now they have to deal with inquisitive looks from the family, and he or she has no idea what has been said about them or how much has been shared about what they are going through. What's equally as troubling is the fact that when the married couple eventually reconciles, they don't always do a good job of relaying that information to the parties they initially shared their problems with. So now here it is two weeks later, and you guys have "kissed and made up" but your in-laws are still giving your spouse the side-eye over what they heard when you guys had a falling out.

When it comes to sharing intimate details of your marriage it is best to have a *Mary and Elizabeth* or a *David and Jonathan* type of friendship. Luke 1:39-56 outlines the relationship that Mary had with Elizabeth. Both women were pregnant during the same time and realized what they were carrying in their wombs was special. They were able to confide in and pray for one another during their pregnancies, as their similarities brought them comfort, peace of mind, and assurance of God's favor.

Likewise, it is better for a married woman to seek guidance and support from another married woman as she tries to navigate the turbulent waters of her marriage. Are we saying that you should never talk with a single woman? Not at all. However, it is more than likely that another married woman has dealt with or is dealing with the same issue, and can provide insight based on their experience.

One of the most famous friendships of the Bible has to be that of David and Jonathan. When they met, David had been chosen by God to be the future king of the Israelites, but Jonathan's father (Saul) who was the king at the time, was extremely jealous of David and wanted to have him killed. However, Jonathan took a real liking to David. He made a promise to him, he loved him, he gave him presents and provided for him. He warned David about plots against him by his father, he spoke out for him to his father and he used his influence to keep him safe. This is the kind of friendship based upon accountability, trust, and honesty, because both parties genuinely have one another's best interest at heart.

Airing Your Dirty Laundry

At the same time one must be mindful when sharing with others that they do not air the 'dirty laundry' of their marriage. Airing out your dirty laundry in your marriage is not healthy. In fact, it can be very damaging to your relationship. It is important to take steps to safeguard your relationship. Some couples just seem to recklessly announce to the world all of the issues and problems that exist in their marriage. It seems like everyone has a backstage pass to the intimate details of their life, from the financial problems to issues with the children or the in-laws, which really should be placed at the altar rather than at the feet of anyone who is willing to listen.

Couples like this tend to talk about one another negatively and don't have secure enough boundaries to protect their marriage. Letting other people's opinions and ideas influence your private relationship is unhealthy. It can break down the marriage as it is no longer a partnership but instead more like a group. Learning how to keep private issues private is important to your marriage.

What Things Should be Kept Private?

At times, it can be difficult to know, what sorts of things to keep private. It is important to have conversations about this as a couple. A lot of what someone thinks should be kept private seems to depend on how they grew up. For example, if someone grew up in a family where money was never discussed, it may seem absurd to talk to friends about how much you just paid for your new house. Meanwhile, for their spouse, talking about money may not seem like a big deal. It would be important for a couple to talk about whether or not they are comfortable sharing about issues such as finances. Make sure to discuss the importance of not discussing your problems to others.

Telling friends and family when you have a fight, the sort of sexual problems you have, or the annoying habits your spouse has is not healthy. Make your expectations clear to your spouse and agree not to air out your dirty laundry to others. Imagine working together to build a fence that will protect your relationship and keep bad things out. This is what you are essentially doing when you maintain privacy within the marriage.

Dangers of Not Maintaining Privacy

Complaining to friends and family about your spouse is disrespectful to your spouse. If you and your spouse are having problems, it is important that the two of you work it out together without the negative influence of others. When you talk to others, keep in mind that misery loves company. If you talk to a friend who is also having marital problems or who has recently gone through a divorce, they may influence you in a way that is not in the best interest to your marriage. Even if they don't consciously say, *"ditch the loser so we can spend time together,"* they may not be able to give you objective advice.

Even if you talk to someone who isn't having any problems of their own, remember that they are only hearing your side of the story. If you go to your friend to say, *"Listen to what happened today with my spouse,"* or *"My spouse treats me in a way I don't like,"* the listener is only hearing your version. Your spouse may have a completely different side of the story.

Telling others about your marriage breaks down the trust in your relationship. If you complain about your spouse to others, you are not honoring the sanctity of the relationship. It is important to protect your spouse, build your spouse up, and remain loyal.

Maintaining Privacy with Technology

Technological advances have made it easier than ever to share your every waking move. Sharing negative information about your relationship on social media sites is not a good idea. Avoid airing out your dirty laundry on Facebook, twitter, a blog, or via text message. If you are angry or upset with your spouse, hold off on announcing anything to the world. It's understandable to be upset when people try to pry into your personal life, but who do you blame when you carelessly give people the fuel and ammunition to sabotage your relationship? The responsibility for that lies solely with you.

Even if you aren't directly saying "*my spouse is a jerk*" in a public forum, posting about your life or family can still be quite revealing. Avoid the passive-aggressive, less direct approach to complaining about your spouse online as well. Advertising something such as "*hopefully my husband is actually home on time for once*," is telling. Remember that jokes and sarcasm don't translate well either, so even if you are just kidding, others may not understand this.

Deciding When to Share

There may be times that you genuinely want to seek the counsel of others. If you need help learning how to communicate or work through problems with your spouse, consider getting professional help. A marriage counselor or a clergy person can assist you in talking about your marital issues in confidence.

When sharing issues with anyone about your marriage, it is important to ask, *"Would I say this if my spouse were right here next to me?"* If the answer is no, don't say it. Part of building a healthy, trusting marriage means that you don't do anything hurtful to your spouse, even when your spouse isn't around.

Two Sides to Every Story

Your marriage is on the rocks. Your spouse is emotionally unavailable and you strongly suspect that they are having an affair. Your spouse never wants to have sex. You are so miserable about your home life you can't even concentrate at work. Things have become so desperate that divorce starts looking like a reasonable option, but you're just not sure what to do. So, you turn to your friends and family for a shoulder to lean on. You tell them about the problems in your marriage and how your spouse just doesn't understand you or your needs.

You share the many ways in which your spouse is selfish, insensitive, deceitful, and controlling and how he or she is completely unwilling to change. Support and empathy is what you're after and you talk about your predicament to any friend or family member with a sympathetic ear. The advice you get feels right, *"I can't believe they treat you that way. You shouldn't put up with it,"* or *"Your wife doesn't deserve you. You are so good to her and she is so self-absorbed."* Vindicated and bolstered, you leave these conversations feeling better. You're right, your spouse is wrong. And that's all that you really wanted to hear.

Weeks turn into months or years and nothing changes in your marriage. With each passing day, you grow increasingly unhappy. Now, your marital beefs become your daily mantra; you've looped your loved ones in on the on-going saga of a marriage gone wrong. Soon, they start wondering, *"What did that jerk do to you today?"* Eventually, you're being urged to cut your losses and get out of your marriage. Your friends and family can't stand to see you hurt any longer. They want you to get on with your life. *"Enough is enough,"* they say, and start offering suggestions about divorce attorneys. And as you're about to see, while it may feel comforting to know that there are people who love, support and understand you, relying on family and friends in this way can easily backfire.

For starters, when you discuss your marital issues with close friends and family, they hear only your side of the story, which by definition, is incomplete and skewed. But this doesn't stop your loved ones from diagnosing your spouse as the problem. Their loyalty to you blinds them from seeing or understanding the context in which the marital problems have developed over time.

Because of their loyalty to you, they often fail to recognize how maybe, it was your actions that may have triggered your spouse to respond or behave in undesirable ways. That's because YOU might be unaware of your own contribution to your relationship struggles as well. As a result, it has become difficult for you to differentiate the forest from the trees.

But beside the fact that your cronies may be shortsighted and biased in terms of your perspective on things, there is an even more problematic twist when it comes to turning to loved ones for support during marital strife. And here it is. YOU MIGHT

CHANGE YOUR MIND ABOUT YOUR SPOUSE. If your spouse starts being kinder, more considerate, loving, involved, sexier, communicative...and so on, you're encouraged and can't wait to share your good news with your inner circle.

Now herein lies the problem. Once things start to improve between you and your spouse, those same people you confided in will not be impressed. As a matter of fact, they are now skeptical or filled with contempt as a result of hearing about how bad your spouse was treating you. Now they say things like, *"Can't you see that he's just trying to manipulate you?" "She's on her best behavior, but it won't last." "Once a cheater/liar, always a cheater/liar." "You've been wanting to get out of your marriage and now you are being brainwashed to stay."* They're frustrated and angry because you've leaned on them and basked in their emotional support, and now, you want to stay married and work things out!! To them it's simply unacceptable.

So, you try to explain that things are different now. You give examples of all the thoughtful things your spouse is doing to show they care. But they won't budge. You just don't understand why they're so stubbornly clinging to their negative views of your spouse. Why aren't they happy for you that your marriage has turned a corner? Why don't they see the changes in your spouse?

And if they really loved you, regardless of what they think about your spouse, shouldn't they just want you to be happy- even if they don't agree with your decisions? This is why it is so much better to confide in people whom you trust, preferably one person who you can confide in. Having an accountability partner means that this is not only someone you trust, but someone who is invested in you, your husband, and your marriage. They are able to speak to you objectively and lovingly point out the truths that you might have overlooked due to your emotions.

These are the people who will listen to you, cry with you, and more importantly…they will pray with you. They will intercede on your behalf even when you are unable to talk or spend time with them on a regular basis. They are able to do this because they understand that maybe, just maybe, God has a different plan than what you are considering for yourself, and for your marriage.

Praying for Your Spouse

Believe it or not, there are many Christian couples that do not take the time to pray together. There are men who flat out refuse to pray with their wives. They would much rather pray by themselves, because praying with their wife makes them feel weird and uncomfortable. Needless to say, that these views are not uncommon. Very few Christian couples actually take the time to pray together. Pollster George Barna recently reported his findings from interviews with 3,142 randomly selected adults, 1,220 of whom were born-again Christians. Here are the results of his poll:

- Of those who are non-Christian, 23% have seen their marriage go through a divorce.
- 27% of those who call themselves born-again Christians have been divorced.
- Of those who label themselves "Fundamentalist Christians," 30% have experienced a divorce.

Prayer is both an indication of devotion and an expression of intimacy. When we follow Christ fully, we must pray. We must make God a priority in this area – especially with the rampant busyness of today's culture. To some couples, praying together is a foreign concept. We have found it to be both essential *and* enjoyable. When we pray together, we metaphorically and physically align ourselves, and place our entire focus on God. Prayer unifies us in purpose as we express thanks to God, bring our problems to Him, and ask Him for guidance.

Prayer unites you spiritually before God.

> Matthew 18:18-20
> (18) "Truly I say to you, whatever you shall bind on earth shall be bound in heaven; and whatever you loose on earth shall be loosed in heaven.
> (19) "Again I say to you, that if two of you agree on earth about anything that they may ask, it shall be done for them by My Father who is heaven.
> (20) "For where two or three have gathered together in My name, there I am in their midst."

We have not met a married couple yet that did not have problems of some type. Some couples have money problems, or in-law problems, or problems with each other, or problems with their children; the list goes on and on. If we as married couples are having this many problems, why aren't we praying together about them? Matthew 18:19 shows how much power a praying couple can have: *"that if two of you agree on earth about anything that they may ask, it shall be done for them by My Father who is heaven."* How much do you think you and your spouse could accomplish if you prayed together daily? What would happen to the amount of problems you face as a married couple if you prayed together about them daily? What kind of adults will your children grow into if the two of you prayed together for them daily? Now can you see why it is extremely imperative for a married couple to pray for-and-with one another on a daily basis?

When you and your spouse hold hands and pray together, you are coming before God as a couple. It is not just you praying and it is not just your spouse praying, but the two of you praying together. You are united spiritually before God as a team. You are now operating on the level that God intended for couples to operate on. You are unified, joined together as one, partners together before God. Praying as a couple is sweet perfume to God.

> John 17:20-26
> (20) "I do not ask in behalf of these alone, but for those also who believe in Me through their word;
> (21) that they may all be one; even as Thou, Father, art in Me, and I in Thee, that they also may be in Us; that the world may believe that Thou didst send Me.
> (22) "And the glory which Thou hast given Me I have given to them; that they may be one, just as We are one;
> (23) I in them, and Thou in Me, that they may be perfected in unity, that the world may know that Thou didst send Me, and didst love them, even as Thou didst love Me.
> (24) "Father, I desire that they also, whom Thou hast given Me, be with Me where I am, in order that they may behold My glory, which Thou hast given Me; for Thou didst love

> Me before the foundation of the world.
> (25) "O righteous Father, although the world has not known Thee, yet I have known Thee; and these have known that Thou didst send Me;
> (26) and I have made Thy name known to them, and will make it known; that the love wherewith Thou didst love Me may be in them, and I in them."

Jesus prayed for unity among his followers. What kind of example does this give to praying couples? The answer is unity. There is strength in unity, and prayer is the glue that strongly bonds a praying couple together. When you pray together as a couple, it is the perfect time to pray for each other's needs. As a married Christian couple, we understand the importance of prayer in our relationship, and when we pray for one another, it reinforces that knowledge.

When your spouse hears you pray, it will let them know what aspects of your life (and the marriage) concern you and it shows them how to pray for you. It may even surprise you to hear your spouse pray for the area of need and concerns that you have been secretly praying for regarding your marriage, the family, and even the finances. Your prayer reveals your heart to God as well as to your spouse.

They will gain a better understanding of who you are just by hearing you speak the sentiments of your heart. You should also listen to what they are praying about as it will inform you of how to better pray for them. It will eventually help the both of you draw strength from praying together. You both will find it enjoyable over time to watch how God answers your joint prayers.

Prayer encourages humility and honesty.

> Luke 18:10-14
> (10) "Two men went up into the temple to pray, one a Pharisee, and the other a tax-gatherer.
> (11) The Pharisee stood and was praying thus to himself, 'God, I thank Thee that I am not like other people: swindlers, unjust, adulterers, or even like this tax-gatherer.
> (12) I fast twice a week; I pay tithes of all I get.'
> (13) But the tax-gatherer, standing some distance away, was even unwilling to lift up his eyes to heaven, but was beating his breast, saying, 'God, be merciful to me, the sinner!'
> (14) "I tell you, this man went down to his house justified rather than the other; for everyone who exalts himself shall be humbled, but he who humbles himself shall be exalted."

Experiencing unity of heart with your spouse is not automatic. It requires a special attitude by both partners. You have to be humble and honest not only with God but also with each other. Jesus taught that an honest and humble heart was an absolute essential for effective prayer when He told the story of the two men who came to the temple to pray. One man was very self-righteous and ended up praying with only himself because God would not hear him. The other man humbled himself and cried out, *"God be merciful to me a sinner!"* Only the second man was received and justified before God, simply because he honestly and humbly confessed his need.

One of the problems that couples have is pride. The result of this pride is the refusal to acknowledge any weaknesses, or needs, to one another. Most of the time we don't even realize how foolish or destructive this can be. However, praying together as a couple is a great way to solve this problem. It is important for you to remember that your spouse knows you and the problems you face better than anyone else in the world. For you to refuse to pray, or to whitewash your problems in prayer, only keeps you further from one another and the depth of relationship you long for.

Therefore, when you pray together, you need to be honest and humble yourself before God. Allow your spouse to hear you confess your needs openly and let your spouse pray for those needs. You can't help but be drawn closer to God and closer to each other as a result.

Prayer develops and deepens your communication.
Good communication is a fundamental key to real companionship and prayer is the hand that turns the key to open this door. If you pray individually and not together as a couple, you tend say things to the Lord that you would never say to each other in casual conversation. But when you learn to pray together as a couple, your spouse will hear you say those intimate things that previously only God heard (provided you are willing to be humble and honest). For example, when a woman hears her husband praying earnestly about his situation at work, she may realize, *Wow, I had no idea this was such a difficult issue for him*. The wife now knows how to better pray for her husband.

After you pray together, it is often a good idea to talk about some the things the two of you were praying about. Use this as an opportunity to learn more about each other. As you learn how to pray with each other, you will also learn how to communicate with each other. You will find that sharing things with God and with each other deepens the level of trust and love that you already have with each other. You have nothing to lose and everything to gain by praying together. Demonstrate your commitment to God by showing Him that you will pray together with your spouse. When you demonstrate your commitment in prayer to obey and follow Christ, you are communicating to your spouse that he/she can trust that you will be committed to fulfilling all your responsibilities in your marriage too. What a sweet fruit of trust and intimacy this will bear.

Your marriage will be built up because you will be built up.
You will never be the loser by giving yourself to pray with your spouse. Scripture makes it clear that when a believer prays he or she will be built up as a result. Jude declared: *"Building yourselves up on your most holy faith, praying in the Holy Spirit"* (Jude 1:20). As you pray and spend time petitioning and communing with the Father, He will build you up. What do you think happens when you pray as a couple? You are built up as a couple. Could your relationship as husband and wife use a little building up? Then pray together. Even if you already have the model marriage, pray together, and make it even better.

If you are one the 92% of Christian couples who do not pray together, you may be wondering how to start praying together. I firmly believe that the husbands should take the lead in this matter. As the spiritual head of the family, it is your responsibility, husbands, to lead. So stop shirking your responsibilities and make the decision to pray together as a couple. Now that you have made the commitment to pray with each other, verbalize that commitment. Tell each other (out loud) that praying together is something that you are going to do and that you will start today. Once you have made that verbal commitment to each other that you will pray as a couple, you have taken the first step.

If you have never prayed together as a couple before, you need to learn how to pray together. At first it may seem awkward and uncomfortable, but it will pass over time. When we first started praying together we were both extremely nervous and uncomfortable, but we managed to get past this stage and we know that you can too. Now that it has become part of our married life, we both miss it greatly when I'm away and we are unable to pray together daily.

Tips on how to start praying together.

Find a mutually agreeable time. This is the best place to begin your conversation with your spouse. Depending on your work schedule, whether or not you have children, and if you and your spouse are morning people like we are, or night owls, you must determine the best time to pray together. Try to determine the most undistracted time of day possible that works for the both of you. Caution: if you and your spouse are not intentional about *making time* for prayer, you will never *find* time for prayer.

After all, you set aside specific time for grooming, eating, and watching special programming every day, so too you will need to set aside time for prayer with your spouse. We would suggest, if you are an early riser, an early morning rendezvous before the kids get up. Or if you are a night person, use that as an opportunity to pray with each other right before you go to bed. **Keep the prayer time short.** One of the mistakes that you can make when beginning a prayer time together is that of trying to immediately pray for an extended period of time. Do not try to impress your spouse with your ability to pray. If your spouse is not accustomed to the practice of prayer, he or she can become turned off to praying with you if you insist on a marathon experience. Don't try to be so spiritual that you end up quenching your partner's desire to pray.

If you want to successfully change your habits, begin with a short time together at first, possibly just a few minutes. This will keep your partner from becoming discouraged, impatient, or intimidated. Let the Lord slowly and naturally lengthen your prayer time together as a result of the Spirit drawing you forward, not by some external rule you have set up.

There are no specific rules to how you pray. No matter who decides to start off the prayer, you both can take turns going back and forth until one partner doesn't pray anymore, or you can take turns leading prayer. Monday, Wednesday and Friday could be designated for your husband, and the other days in between could be for your wife. No matter what you decide, just remember that God will bless your marriage through prayer. You just have to be willing to take the first step, and He will meet you both there.

Effective Communication

The most commonly reported problem in marriages by far is communication. This may be one of the broadest and most difficult terms to define with regard to marriages. It tends to have many different meanings to each of us. For the purpose of this explanation we will define it as "*Misunderstanding*". Most dictionaries define this word as the failure to understand something on someone correctly. Literally, this means not being able to understand the other person's point of view. This is often more a matter of refusing to allow the existence of the other's view as opposed to not understanding it.

It is an unwillingness to take the time to genuinely listen and care to understand. In many relationships the interest seems to lie primarily in getting one's own point of view heard and understood rather than having an interest in hearing and understanding the other person. There is a subtle irony here worth looking at. If people cared to listen to the other person with as much interest as he or she wished the other would listen to them, both of them would end up receiving exactly what they are looking for!

To truly know another, we must be willing to see the world through their eyes, not simply our own. If we listened as well as we spoke, really connecting would take care of itself . . .

Created for Communication

Human beings were created for communication, especially in marriage. Of all places, marital communication should reflect the intimate and harmonious communication of God Himself. For God is a Trinity — *Father, Son*, and *Holy Spirit*—the only true and perfect Communication from all eternity. Whatever intimate and harmonious communication is, it is found perfectly in the Trinity. We are created in God's image. So we were created for communication, communication that is designed for beauty, intimacy, and harmony. Of all places, this should be best expressed in our Christian marriages.

Barriers to Communication

What makes marital communication so difficult? Basically, we all face specific barriers that hinder a deepening communication in our marriages. First, we all carry some baggage with us from our upbringing. Our parents may have never communicated with each other or with us.

They may have told us that children are to be seen and not heard. Second, we live in an isolating culture. Things like television, the Internet, and video games isolate us from those nearest and dearest to us. We get comfortable finding our own meaning, purpose, and values without having to interact and communicate with others. Third, we are bombarded with outside pressures. Jobs, car pools, church meetings, and the like, can steal the quality time needed for real communication between husbands and wives. Fourth, we tend to be lazy, gravitating to the nearest comfort zone. Real marital communication takes time, effort, and planning. It is not for the fainthearted. And fifth, we may be fearful of showing our emotions or of being rejected if we communicate openly and honestly.

It can't be stated often enough. If you don't have a healthy way of expressing your thoughts and emotions to each other, of speaking and being heard, then everything else will ultimately crumble. In order to have a successful marriage you have to make yourself an expert in communication. You have to try to understand what your partner is saying on a simple level as well as try to analyze the underlying message or desire.

The last thing a woman wants to hear when she complains about her weight is a suggestion for a new diet plan. For example, when a wife is standing in front of the closet deciding what outfit to wear, may not be the best time for her husband to shift the conversation to the additional weight she gained over the holidays. Nor does she want just a sympathetic ear (just when a man thinks he's mastered the art of good listening).

She is already aware of the additional weight she put on, and she understands the benefit of eating healthier and working out on a regular basis. What she really wants is for her husband to say, *"You look beautiful!" "You look amazing!" "I love how you look!"* This is the underlying message, the motivation behind the communication. We all need to be amateur psychologists and try to figure out what our partner really wants.

For example, when Tasha tells her husband that she isn't feeling well, that may be her way of saying *"could you drive the children to school today honey?"* or it may be her way of expressing a need for more attention from her spouse. It should be noted that we can't all be mind-readers. That is why we need to try to focus not just on the words being said, but what may possibly be implied as well. It is important to hear what your spouse is really saying, and it is equally as important for the other side to give clues. We shouldn't expect our spouses to intuit our needs nor rely on some level of divine inspiration. If there's a special necklace you want for your birthday, point it out to your husband. It will save him the agony of choosing and spare you both needless pain. It works both ways -- maybe he doesn't want socks this year!

Tell Your Spouse What You Want

Troy is the romantic type. Every week after he got engaged he brought his fiancée flowers. He even sent her flowers every day of the week before their wedding. He continued this practice a number of years into their marriage. Finally Keisha, his wife, ever the unsentimental and practical one, spoke up. *"You know Troy, I really love you and I like that you want to bring me flowers. But I actually don't like flowers that much. And besides, they die so soon after that I feel like we've wasted our money. I'd rather you saved up for a more lasting gift."*

Bottom line, if we want something, we need to say it. Luckily this is a very trivial example. But being able to express yourself in the small areas will lead to open discussion in the big areas as well. A closed mouth will never get fed. Even infants cry when they are hungry, because they have no other way to articulate their need. It sounds so obvious, but we have seen many hurt and angry couples come in for counseling saying *"he should have known..."* or *"she should have realized..."* How should he have known? How should she have realized, if you never took the time to tell them?

Listen to Your Spouse

In 2015, we became certified PAIRS counselors. PAIRS is an acronym which stands for *Practical Application of Intimate Relationship Skills*. During our training, we discovered that one of the more important (and most neglected) forms of communication in a relationship, was the discipline of being an active listener.

Sometimes when you and your spouse are quarreling, one of you need to stop and ask: *"What am I saying, and what are you saying, and are we really listening to each other?"* It may sound simple, but it can be very effective. God gave us two ears and only one mouth, probably so we could listen twice as much as we speak! You see, sometimes you can find yourself so caught up in hearing yourself talk or the passion of the moment that you haven't really been listening to your spouse. You will be amazed to discover that your positions aren't that far apart, in fact they're not apart at all.

If this is a difficult issue for you it sometimes helps to establish structure. You could set aside a time where you are required to listen to your spouse without interrupting for 10 minutes. Don't plan your defense or rebuttal. Just listen. You'll be surprised at how much you'll learn and when it's your turn you'll realize a unique pleasure in being able to express yourself freely.

Another technique we like to use in our PAIRS counseling is called active listening. It is one thing to hear someone talking, and another thing altogether to listen to what they are saying. There are many variations on this theme but the basic style is mirroring back what your partner says. *"I hear you saying..."*

Keep doing it until you get it right. Maybe many of your misunderstandings are because you heard your spouse wrong the first time, or you didn't hear them at all. It all comes back to being intentional about listening to your spouse, and not just hearing them.

We have numerous distractions in our lives today, from cell phones, tablets, televisions, and the Internet. If we want to be listened to with concentration, we must be willing to turn them off when necessary. Let the person you are talking to on the phone know that you will call them back, because your spouse has just arrived home from work. It will not kill you to turn off ESPN for a few minutes, or the latest reality television show long enough to prioritize the needs of your spouse and your family. It can be disheartening to roll over in the middle of the night to snuggle with your spouse, and to see the ultraviolet light from their cell phone beaming on their face. And we wonder where the intimacy has gone?

Taking time to silence the outside distractions of life will show your spouse (and your family) that you are still engaged and invested in them. Otherwise they will begin to feel like they are in competition for your time and attention, and when you have something to say it might end up falling on deaf ears. We have to remember that marriage creates a unity, a kind of oneness. We can use our powers of communication to solidify that unity or we can use them to tear it apart.

True Intimacy

Marital Intimacy – What is it really?

The term "marital intimacy" is a catch phrase that is used frequently in today's culture to politely refer to the act of sexual intercourse. If you attend a couple's seminar, however, you might hear the same phrase used to describe a much broader context of relationship between a husband and a wife. The idea of intimacy implies a connection between two persons, in this case between two spouses.

The writer of the Book of Ecclesiastes speaks of two individuals deriving warmth from lying down together (Ecclesiastes 4:9). The same passage provides a visual picture of a rope that is woven with three strands of cord to symbolize the intimate connection that exists in a marriage that is strengthened by God.

From these verses in the Bible, we can understand that while marital intimacy is certainly about a physical connection, it is much more than that. The Apostle Paul writes in Ephesians 5:31 about a mysterious union of a man who, by joining himself to a wife, becomes one flesh with her. As we study the significance of marital intimacy, we can come to understand the potential for a husband and wife to have a deep, rewarding relationship that encompasses four areas; emotional, mental/social, spiritual, and physical.

Marital Intimacy – How do we experience it?

Marital intimacy can be a deep and rewarding connection between a husband and wife. The real question is, *"How do we experience it?"* Marital Intimacy is accomplished as a husband and wife seek to sacrificially love each other by learning to meet each other's needs within the marriage.

A number of good books have been written on the subject of how to understand the differences between men and women and how to begin to meet each other's needs in marriage. Of course, no spouse should ever be expected to meet all the needs of the other. Nevertheless, each husband and wife team is made up of two large puzzle pieces, that when fit together, will create a beautiful panoramic picture of what marital intimacy is all about.

Marital Intimacy is achieved in all of its completeness as each spouse learns to share and connect with the other in four areas: emotional, mental, spiritual, and physical. Because God, the Creator of mankind, designed men and women uniquely, the way in which these four aspects of intimacy are experienced is somewhat different for each spouse. Women generally seek the fulfillment of emotional connection and want to know that feelings are both valued and shared in an intimate relationship.

They also enjoy communicating closeness through mental forms of intimacy and "feel connected" through a mutual exchange of thoughts. This allows them to enter into the daily world where their husbands live and think. Men are wired somewhat differently, and tend to experience the greatest levels of intimacy through companionship, activity, and forms of physical intimacy, such as sexual intercourse. While the intimacy needs of women might be described as "being," the same needs in men can best be conceptualized as "doing."

Marital Intimacy – Where does God fit in?

Intimacy occurs when two people in marriage—without reservation—draw close to each other spiritually, emotionally and physically creating oneness. God designed for us to be intimate on all three of those levels. You are most vulnerable at your weakest link. Sadly, affairs can begin in church in the choir loft simply because you are sitting next to a person who is more intimate with you spiritually. Perhaps they are praying with you and concerned about spiritual things more than your own spouse is. Spiritual intimacy is vital to the success of your marriage.

Here are some ways you can love your marriage through increase spiritual intimacy:

1. Go to church with your spouse.
2. Read the Bible together.
3. Join a Bible study, the choir, or volunteer together through something your church is doing.

Discover why certain spiritual things are important to them by asking questions like, "Tell me what's going on there. Why is that important to you? If your wife or your husband has spiritual interests, you need to be interested too. The further you are apart emotionally, intellectually, spiritually, the more vulnerable you are for someone else to come in and connect with your spouse to meet that need for spiritual intimacy. Remember, intimacy begins with the spiritual connection.

A woman experiences the deepest intimate connection with her husband through emotional validation and mental exchange. A man achieves the same feeling of intimacy through involvement with his wife in behaviors that enhance closeness. Physical intimacy is a significant part of achieving that closeness. A husband and a wife can be intimately involved in meeting each other's emotional, mental, and physical needs.

What about the spiritual aspect of marital intimacy? Where does God fit in? He waits to be invited to become the third cord spoken of in Ecclesiastes, Chapter 4. God reveals Himself in the opening chapters of Genesis, the first book of the Bible, as Creator of the universe and of mankind. Here, we find that God has created human beings in His image. This means that men and women are "soulish" people. In other words, we have a human spirit that was made to connect with the Spirit of the living God. God intends that we also join our spirits together within the covenant of marriage.

How do we achieve spiritual intimacy? We must first recognize God as the One who has created us and designed a spiritual life for us. Once we have entered into a personal relationship with Him, then we are ready to share our spiritual journey with our spouse as we seek all that God has for us within the beautiful covenant of Godly marriage.

While physical intimacy is essential, the heart of a marriage is the emotional connection (otherwise sex can become a duty, necessary evil, and conjure up resentment—typically to the wife).

If emotional intimacy is so important, how can you maintain it in your marriage? Romans chapter 12 highlights two actions you can take to keep the intimacy in your marriage: love genuinely and give preference to one another.

Love Genuinely (Romans 12:9)

In ancient Greece, the word "hypocrisy" was used to describe those who acted in stage plays. In essence, they were pretending to be someone they were not in real life, so they were called hypocrites. The same is true in marriage. Pretending to love your spouse is a quick way to zap the intimacy from your marriage (not to mention you will eventually end up being exposed as a fraud).

You may be wondering how you can be hypocritical in your love towards your spouse. Well, one way is to do things with an ulterior motive or to set your spouse up for a fall, while seemingly appearing to care for him/her. Another way to love hypocritically is to say one thing, yet have a completely different intention in your heart. Obviously, this weakens your marriage. So, to keep the flame burning in your marriage, you will have to be genuine in your love.

Give Preference to One Another (Romans 12:10)

The second way to keep intimacy in your marriage is to give preference to your spouse. When we hear the word preference, a picture that should come to mind is pulling up to a parking spot at the same time as another car. While you may want to quickly park your car so you will get the closest spot, you find yourself intentionally letting the other person take the spot. Sure, it means you have to keep hunting, and perhaps walk a longer distance, but it also allows you to put someone else first.

In your marriage, you'll have a number of opportunities to put yourself first, second, and third, with your spouse coming in at a distant fourth. While we are not suggesting you deny your well-being or health for your spouse's sake, we are advising that you actively look for ways that you can put your spouse first. For instance, some women believe that their husband is always wired for sex. This is not always true. Having a healthy sex-drive does not necessarily equate to wanting sex every day.

As a wife, you should hold the key to his heart as well as the key to the ignition of his engine. You should know what it takes to "start him up" and you should also know when his engine has been overworked, and he needs an "oil change". In contrast, a husband must be just as considerate of his wife's libido. Coming home, tossing your suitcase on the couch, grabbing your wife around the waist while proceeding to tongue-her-down, is not the most romantic prelude to an intimate evening. A husband must learn how to tap into his wife's mind as well as her body, and find new ways of stimulating her on an intellectual level. For some women it's relaxing while reading a book by the fireplace. For another it might be just sitting on the deck with a glass of wine while you both share the details of your day.

Giving preference to one another will lead to reciprocity, and it will enhance the intimacy in your marriage dramatically, as you both will feel appreciated and loved. To review, emotional intimacy is oxygen to a relationship, and without it, your marriage will slowly die. These actions will help your marriage maintain the emotional intimacy it needs to burn long and hot.

Section Two Questions

1. **Do you recognize the need for discretion when it comes to your marriage?**

2. **Do you pray for your spouse? Why?**

3. **Describe the ways in which you and your wife can communicate better.**

4. **What are your thoughts on intimacy and your marriage?**

Notes

"What couples need to understand, is that it is okay to be open and willing to share certain aspects of their marriage in public. All relationships go through challenges of some sort, and these challenges can either make the relationship stronger or tear it apart. We believe it is important to surround yourself with married couples who are not afraid of sharing the good, the bad and the ugly, especially if it helped them make it to a better place in their relationship. What gives people hope about going through rough patches in their marriage, are the stories about couples who have been there and done that, and can speak from a place of wholeness. My husband and I believe it is a blessing to be able to encourage other married couples through words or pictures of us being happy or just living life. People need to see more fun-loving marriages and we don't mind sharing what God has blessed us with."

- Billy & Irene Council-Grant

Representing Your Spouse

One of the joys of being married is that you have someone (in the person of your spouse) that has your back and your best interest at heart. Unfortunately we see that many couples have no real understanding of what that is. Somehow they think that *"keeping it real"* or *"keeping it 100"* means that any kind of behavior is acceptable. Marriage is not only a partnership, but it is a representation of Christ and one another.

Each marriage is different and has its own personality, which is crafted by both the husband and the wife. The characteristics of a healthy marriage are comprised of the values and principles that drive it. It is not enough for a husband and wife to represent the values and principals they share when they are behind closed doors.

It speaks volumes when both of them are able to become the embodiment of those same values and principals when they are out in public. How does a husband represent his wife when he is out-and-about in public settings when she is not around? How does a wife carry herself in public settings when she is around the opposite sex? Public representation of your spouse when they are not in your presence is extremely important. Proverbs 31:23 talks about how a husband is *"respected at the city gate"* because of how she carries herself. As a wife, how do you carry yourself at work and other public places when your husband is not around? Are men who know you are married (and even know your husband) inclined to engage in certain conversation with you because you demonstrate that it is ok?

As a husband, how do you carry yourself outside of your wife's presence? Are you flirtatious with the receptionist at your job or do you make off-color comments to that young lady who happens to be a personal trainer at the local gym? If your wife just happened to accompany you one day to the gym or if she dropped off lunch at your job, would those women feel the need to "adjust" how they speak with you now that your wife is there?

These are some of the questions that need to be answered when a married couple considers how they represent God, their marriage, and one another in public. Let us take a closer look.

Here are 5 characteristics that a husband and wife should represent in public.

Honesty

Representing your spouse in the spirit of honesty gives people an idea of who you are and what kind of person your spouse is. It may not be a fair assessment of your spouse, but people only know what you show them or what they have heard about you.

For example, when you are not with your spouse are you prone to lie? Do you keep your word? Do you compromise the truth for the sake of manipulating people and/or situations? When people see that you are someone who is dishonest in your dealings with them, they will begin to wonder if your spouse is the same way. Make sure you a representing your marriage in public with honesty and integrity, especially when your spouse is not around.

Protective

Representing your spouse means that you are intentional about protecting them. You will not allow your friends, family, or even your own mother to disrespect them. When your spouse has your back, it means they will defend you and will not allow others to harm you. This means speaking highly of you when your name comes up in conversation.

It means that you willingly celebrate their achievements and you express how much you appreciate what they do for you and your family. Now if you know you have married someone who is not currently living up to the standard of being a good spouse, then don't say anything at all. That is always better than throwing them under the bus.

Supportive

Representing your spouse also means being supportive. Even if you are not in total agreement of their latest idea or career endeavor, never shoot them down in front of people. Yes it can be difficult to hide your pessimism when it comes to certain things, especially if you both have been down this road before. It's easy to point to a recent failure in order to avoid trying the same thing again, but God sometimes uses several "No's" in your spouse's life in order to develop their resilience.

The fact that you are still supportive of them in the face of great odds, will cause their faith to increase. What a great witness it is to others to see that you hung in there during the lean times and you are now reaping the rewards of the success that was birthed by you simply being supportive. This also means that your spouse will be supportive you, even if they don't understand you. You may have certain things that you are passionate about that your spouse just doesn't understand or like. But when your spouse has your back, they will support you in reaching your goals even if they don't always understand them.

Team Player

Representing your spouse means that you are willing to defer and to compromise when necessary. Not getting 100% of what you want at the exact time that you want it, doesn't mean your spouse doesn't have your back. Sometimes they may have valuable insight that you do not have which allows them to make an informed decision. Marriage is about give and take. It is about recognizing your strength and acknowledging your weaknesses.

It means not being insecure when you have to "stay in your own lane" because your spouse is able to do something better than you. When you truly have each other's back, you will work together as a team to make things happen.

Trustworthy

Last but not least, representing your spouse means that you can depend on them. If your spouse is not dependable and can't be trusted, you will feel more like you are watching your own back rather than like your back is being watched. A spouse that has your back is one who is right behind you and is there to protect and cover you.

This provides you with the greatest sense of security in public. When you are not in their presence you are able to make informed decisions simply because you know that you have a trusted partner at home. There is no fear or insecurity about who they are and who you are to them.

Here are some final thoughts on how a husband and wife should represent one another in public. A wife who represents her husband well is one who considers how she looks and what she puts on when she leaves the house. She knows that she represents God, her husband, and her family. Beauty is just as much a state of mind as it is what one chooses to wear.

Likewise, a husband must also consider what kind of message he's conveying when he's out-and-about in public. What kind of attention is he bringing to himself, and is there a pattern being repeated? What kind of conversation does he engage in when his wife is not around? Does he even mention his wife and children when he has a conversation with another female? Does he mention his love for God?

When spouses represent each other, it means that they can depend on each other and that they are looking out for one another. There is nothing more comforting than knowing that your spouse has you covered…physically and spiritually. The way you represent your spouse in public not only says a lot about how you feel about them, but how you feel about the marriage as a whole.

Public Displays of Affection

Let us first preface our discussion for this chapter by stating that "public displays of affection" are not for everyone. Many people think it is pretty lame to see a couple all over each other in public. If you haven't yelled "get a room" to some couple over the years, then surely you have whispered it under your breath a time or two.

Then there is the couple that tries to walk side by side with each other, both of them having an arm around the others hip. How about the couple that tries to walk one in front of the other with both arms around each other? They have to get this sort of synchronized walking thing down so that they don't trip over each other on every step! Sometimes you can't help but laugh when you see that.

Then there are couples who engage in the passionate, public make-out session, which can be a bit much. Finally, there are the couples (like The Grahams) who publicly display their hugs, kisses, and emphatic *"I love you declarations"* which is enough to cause our children to squirm in their seats if not vomit in their mouth! But wait a minute. Maybe public displays of affection are not all that bad. Maybe they are just abused and misunderstood. Abused by the oblivious few and misunderstood by the conservative majority. Think about it. You were probably far more apt to exhibit these public displays of affection when you first met your husband or wife. Were they not some of the most innocent and fun times you had together in the beginning of your courtship? But now you feel like you're too old now… and since you've been married for so many years…you're pretty much over that now…right? Wrong…or at least you shouldn't be over it.

Most of the happy long term marriages you will ever encounter will each have the same common theme. Almost without fail, the spouses always greet each other with a kiss, just like when they were first dating. Not a kiss that would make everyone else sick around them but a kiss that you can tell is standard in their relationship.

You'll also notice the man finding ways to touch his wife in kind, respectful and uplifting ways. He places a hand on the small of her back as he ushers her into a room or into a chair. She reciprocates by interlocking her arm with his or leaning her head on his shoulder. The list could go on but these are a couple examples of public displays of affection that are not going to make others gag, and at the same time keep the romanticism alive. They keep it young. They keep it fresh.

You have to admit that there is something special about a couple in a crowded room that beeline it to each other after locking eyes for the first time that day. It doesn't matter if they are 90 years old or 20 years old. It is as if no one else in the room matters…and for that brief moment, they have dedicated a few seconds to each other to reconnect. When they kiss…it's not hurried and you can tell they're not embarrassed. It is their moment and they don't care who is watching. They make it magical, and instead of others throwing up, they're left in awe.

What is interesting is that we live in a society where public displays of ratchet behavior and violence are celebrated, while public displays of loving affection are frowned upon. Could the real issue be that people are unhappy with themselves? Could it be that someone who has given up on loving others (let alone loving themselves) now despises the very expressions of love that are displayed in their presence?

What next? People who hand wash their car in public will now be frowned upon by people who would rather take their car to a traditional carwash? Should people who are fans of their favorite sports team refrain from showing their enthusiasm in public after their team wins a ballgame?

Happiness is expressed in many ways, shapes and forms, and it is a universal part of the human experience. Loving your spouse and desiring to express that love is natural. How you choose to express that love, in public and in private, should be your prerogative. For some couples it is as simple as just holding hands or sharing a loving gaze at a restaurant, while for others it might be the occasional peck on the lips.

Nevertheless, if you are in a marriage where your spouse desires some form of public affection, it behooves you to at least consider how you might acquiesce. At the end of the day, only the two of you know if what you are sharing is either a genuine public display of affection, or if it is an attempt to gain public attention.

Marriage and Social Media

Recent research claims that one out of five (20%) divorce cases include some mention of social media related complaints. Indeed, many people have reported ruined marriages stemming from situations in which social networking has played a role. Others are quick to point out that during the same time period of the rapid growth of social networking divorce rates have actually declined slightly (as have marriage rates).

Social media defenders argue that before the technology existed, people utilized every other means available for their infidelity – including email, text messaging, telephones, and so forth. They point to social networking as a tool cheaters use, but not the cause of the problem.

Most conclude that Facebook and similar online networks can be harmless and fun when utilized appropriately. As with anything good, if it is placed in the wrong hands and used with the wrong intent…it can be harmful. It is important to recognize, however, that inappropriate social network participation can indeed be problematic for marriages – not just with infidelity, but in many other areas as well. Couples should be proactive about protecting themselves and their marriages from possible social media pitfalls. *Here are seven practical tips to consider:*

(1) ***Watch the clock***. Spending too much time on any activity can be harmful to your family relationships. But spending an inordinate amount of time engaging in social network activities can be particularly distressing to your spouse. One of the biggest challenges married couples face is finding quality time to spend with each other. Yet, we don't seem to have nearly as much trouble finding time to spend online. If you are not careful, social media can be an addicting time drain.

(2) ***Don't air your dirty laundry***. Facebook, Twitter, and the like are not appropriate venues to post grievances about your spouse or otherwise cause embarrassment. Even updates that are intended to be humorous may not be perceived as such by your spouse. Furthermore, others are not privy to the context to determine if such a post was made in jest or out of spite. Always make it a point to present your marriage in a positive light – whether online or in any other public setting.

(3) ***Share selectively***. Social media makes it fun and easy to share our lives with friends, family, and others. Because of this ease – not to mention the inexplicable, gratifying feeling that it creates – we are often emboldened to share many details about ourselves and our daily goings-on. While this seems innocent and harmless, it actually has the potential to endanger that special intimacy that you should be preserving for your marriage. Be thoughtful about what you share.

(4) ***Establish safeguards together***. You need to be on the same page with your spouse regarding social network options. The only way to do this is to talk about it. Is there current or potential online contacts or "friends" with whom either of you are uncomfortable? Are their certain communication methods that either of you think should be off limits to people of the opposite sex (e.g. email, private message, chat)? What level of personal and family information should be shared online?

(5) ***Exchange passwords***. When you share online passwords with your spouse it reflects trust, openness, commitment, and accountability. It also demonstrates that your online interactions are appropriate and that there is nothing to hide. Why would a married couple not want to share passwords with one another? The answer to that question may be revealing.

(6) ***Leave the past in the past***. It is decidedly unwise to connect with old flames, former love interests, or anyone with whom you have shared a close relationship in the past. Doing so invites an unnecessary threat into your married life. Such threats may include: jealousy, insecurity, or anxiety for your spouse; unwanted advances from the other person; confusing thoughts and emotions; various temptations; and many others. Even if your motive for the connection does not stem from impure intentions it is not worth the risk.

(7) ***Choose your "friends" wisely***. Ultimately, it is your decision and responsibility to determine who you will add to your social media contacts. Once social network connections are made, these people have more access into your life. Remember, you can

always "unfriend" someone whose posts or interactions have become uncomfortable or offensive to you or your spouse. Any online contact that can strain your relationship with your spouse is not a contact worth keeping.

In this chapter we want to focus on something that we have observed over a long period of time since, technology crept in our lives, notably social media, and started transforming our lives from real/actual to 'virtual'. Our lives, and those of others, have been changed and are greatly impacted by social media and virtual communities, more than anyone would have ever imagined!

Virtual relationships are just that; meeting and connecting with people online, nevertheless it is necessary to set boundaries and limits of how you can connect or share with them, and how deep you can go in an online relationship. If you are a social person offline, you may have reservations about making genuine connections with people online.

To feel connected to a person, you want to see them, look in their eyes, share a smile, share an experience, laugh…in short, body language is important in our connections. This, we know, is impossible to achieve online, unless plans are ahead to meet in person. That is our personal opinion, which could hold true most but not all the time; we have made great online friendships and we know of great relationships that brewed online.

Another thing that makes many people skeptical about social media and virtual communities is that the interactions are more private than online ones. There is little or no privacy in the online world, and anything said in a social forum, no matter how discreet or secret the forum claims to be, is subject to publicity. Which brings us to how most people; especially women are using social networks to share their lives with their virtual communities.

Thanks to technology, our relationships have increased, and we can belong to as many virtual communities as we can. We can also talk out our hearts, share our joys/worries, recipes, parenting advice, family planning advice, and the list is endless. But it is the marital affairs that are being aired mostly on social media, which is a bit alarming.

Every day, we see women disclosing their marital troubles with members of their virtual communities. Mostly, these troubles are aired in forms of complaints or regrets, and therefore it is only human, and imperative that they share them out to a party willing to listen. Unfortunately, airing your marital troubles online is problematic because you might be dealing with a temporary issue that ends up being permanent issue for those people following you online. Think about it.

The same people who post about their cheating spouse, often neglect to post about how they went to counseling, prayed and worked through their issues and after three months they are doing better. So in essence, their followers are left holding on to the issue that that was posted months ago, and have now formed a permanent opinion about the situation. It is both unfair and inadequate to make an impartial judgment when you have only one side of the story - a story has two sides. It's only when we have the whole story, or more so if the parties involved are known to us, that we can be able to make a sound judgment.

Sometimes, we do not know the intention of the person while posting; whether they need sympathy, solutions, or they want someone simply to take sides with them as a way of approving their feelings/opinions/decisions. Sometimes, the issues aired are, with all due respect, petty and can be solved with the help of the spouse concerned without involving a third party.

There are no universal rules or guidelines that govern marriage, therefore you cannot employ what works in your friend's marriage and expect it to work in your own. Every marriage is different, and so are the parties in it, so applying a one-size fits all may be doing more harm than good to a marriage.

Perhaps it is wise to do a SWOT (Strengths, Weaknesses, Opportunities, and Threats) of your marriage to know where improvement is needed, how the strengths can be used to improve the weakness and opportunities to counter the threats. Every marriage has its own personality and unique make-up. What may be viewed as a strength in Vicki & Ray's marriage may be a form of weakness in Martin & Tenita's marriage. Just as the four individuals are different, so is their marriage.

Are we saying that you should never share your concerns with others? Certainly not, however, you should always consider with whom you are sharing, what you are sharing, and why you are sharing.

> ***1).*** *Have a personal friend, preferably not of the opposite sex, if possible, one who knows your spouse well but does not socialize with him regularly. This one is a must; she should be* ***married*** *and be* ***for marriage****. It is in your best interest to avoid emotional affairs that mainly commence, unintentionally or intentionally, when we confide in our opposite sex friends. You also want to make sure that your best friends/family are not hearing about your marital problems and not inquiring from you.*

2). *Have an agreed upon* ***mutual couple*** *(let's call them a mentor couple) that you can confide in, the two of you, when you need help. Make sure that your chosen friend is an* ***empathetic*** *listener, one you can verbalize your concerns to and understand them well. Your friend should be someone discreet, has you and your spouse's interests at heart, who is both ethical and able to remain objective.*

3). *If possible, avoid sharing infidelity issues with your friends or family, no matter how difficult it may sound. Sharing your spouse's unfaithfulness with them may harbor in them negative feelings towards him or her, and may be a hindrance in saving your marriage.*

4). *Never keep your marital problems, no matter how minor they may be, to yourself. Instead, choose, very carefully and wisely, a 'safe' personal friend or two, to whom you can confide in.*

Always remain loyal while doing so, and never share things about your spouse that you wouldn't want him to share with others about you, since no one is perfect. When sharing on social media always be mindful to not blatantly throw your spouse under the bus. Be careful to filter the information you post, keeping in mind that your marriage is not an episode of reality television.

Be intentional about creating a safe place for your spouse to share the sentiments of their heart. Handle your personal issues in public with the care and compassion that you would want them to show you in public. Ask yourself how your spouse would feel if they discovered how you strip them of loyalty and dignity and discuss about them with strangers, who have never met them.

Ask yourself whether, if they learn about your disloyalty, they would feel guarded to share anything with you, since you will go and share with others. We're not saying you can't tell *anyone* about your marital problems, we're saying that you don't have to tell *everyone*. Never share with outsiders things about your marriage that you haven't talked to your spouse about. It may feel better to do so, but at the end of the day, it will only make things worse.

Why are we placing so much emphasis on this you ask? To be quite honest, it is because the introduction of social media into our lives has forced the church to identify what is acceptable and unacceptable. The church must be careful to remain prophetic and relevant in a world where truth is often rejected and lies are more readily embraced.

We believe that the greatest danger to the purity of the church is when it allows itself to become conformed to the things of the world. We are called to *live in the world* but not *be of the world.* Too often we have seen how the church has been quick to embrace the trends and influences of secular society, while compromising its own integrity. The church must prioritize speaking and walking in truth if it wants to remain a prophetic and relevant voice in this world. Therefore, make sure you govern yourself accordingly when using social media.

The Court of Public Opinion

If you've been dealing with some problems in your marriage, you may be wondering if you should confide in a friend or family member. We all need to talk about our problems from time to time, but it's important to be very selective about what you discuss with other people. Did you know that talking about issues that you're having in your marriage or complaints that you have with your spouse, may only make things worse? Here are some reasons why you should think twice before telling others about problems in your marriage.

1. No Resolution

Most people don't feel that any harm can be done by talking about their marital problems. Usually they just want advice on how to resolve the problems that they are having. Sometimes they're simply looking for someone to listen to them, while they express their frustrations.

Perhaps they just want reassurance that everything will be okay. Even if you have the best of intentions, talking about the problems in your marriage may not resolve anything. You may spend hours discussing the problem only to find out that nothing gets fixed.

2. Your Spouse May Find out and Feel Betrayed

Your spouse may not want other people to know about things that go in your marriage. They may feel that conversations regarding your marriage are private and should only be discussed between the two of you.

Most married couples have said negative things about their spouse to someone else at one time or another. None of us are perfect. However, it behooves us to guard our emotions when we are sharing details about our spouse or our marriage. It is never a good look to throw your spouse under the bus. An emotional tirade is a golden opportunity for the enemy to exploit the vulnerabilities that exist in your marriage.

3. It's Impossible to Get an Objective Point of View

Asking for advice from someone who is mutually invested or who may somehow benefit from your involvement in a particular situation is problematic. How can you totally trust what they're saying when their intent is to remain agreeable so that they do not come out on the short-end of your decision? Also, speaking to your mother or sister about the problems in your marriage will be a challenge, because it will be difficult to receive an objective opinion. Your family loves you and will be more likely to side with you. Even if it seems like someone is being objective, you should be careful of what you say. When you ask their opinion you're opening the door for them to express their feeling and concerns about your marriage and you may not like what they have to say. You may find that they have never liked your spouse and completely disagree with the choices you've made. They may also feel that they have the right to express their concerns about your marriage in the future, even if you don't ask for their advice.

4. It May Become Public Knowledge

If you tell your mom about an issue in your marriage, she may feel like there's no harm in telling your dad or your grandma about the situation. If they decide to tell other people, you may have friends or acquaintances calling you to see what's going on in your marriage. This could leave you very upset with your mother and other members of your family.

When you can, try to remember to only tell people information that you don't mind others knowing. It's also best to avoid talking to anyone about your problems who has a tendency to blow things out of proportion.

5. You Could Get Bad Advice

When you ask for someone's advice, it may not be what you want to hear. The person you ask may have a negative outlook on marriage because of their own situation. This may cause them to give you bad advice without meaning to. Also, if you're speaking with someone who doesn't like your spouse, they're likely to give you bad advice too.

Always be careful if you think that the person you're speaking with could be in a similar situation because your conversation may cause them to start thinking that they have problem in their own marriage. There may also be times when the person you confide in feels that you are in the wrong and if you're not careful it could cause you to have hurt feelings toward them as well. It is always best to seek God in whom to confide in, as He will lead you to the right person at the right place, and at the right time.

6. You're Not Presenting a United Front

While we agree that it doesn't matter what others think about your marriage, it is not good for people to think that your marriage is on the rocks. When you constantly bad mouth your husband or complain about problems that you have, it doesn't take long for people to start thinking that your marriage is in trouble.

After a while, you may start to think that you have a bad marriage too. This could lead to disagreements that with your spouse that could have been avoided. When you present a united front and people see that you are happily married, they're less likely to attempt to cause problems in your marriage.

Other people can be the death of your relationship. Not just your wife's ex-boyfriend who still sends the occasional text message or that cute waitress who always flirts with your husband, but we mean the people closest to you – the well-meaning, opinionated friends and family members who can systematically tear your relationship apart … if you let them.

Often, the reasons that people choose to leave or stay in relationships are someone else's – either because we are trying to mimic their relationships, take their advice or live up to their standards. These "other people" are not insignificant, but they are insignificant when deciding what kind of marriage you want to have. This is not to say that you should tell your parents or other loved ones to mind their own business and never give you advice.

It's important to know your history, which includes where you come from and the perspectives of the people you come from. Discuss what they think and how they developed those perspectives and values. There could be useful information there. However, their word is not the gospel. While the person advising you could be 100-percent correct in his/her own case, or even in most cases, the advice may not be 100-percent correct for you at this point in your life.

Some years ago, before we developed some of our current relationships philosophies, a friend asked us for advice about his tumultuous marriage. He and his wife fought all the time, and he was very unhappy. Believe it or not, we regurgitated all of the classic clichés and things that had been regurgitated to us over the years: *"Marriage is forever. Stay for the kids. You can make it work."* He looked at us like we were crazy and pursued getting a divorce anyway. Today, he and his ex-wife are both much happier, and at the end of the day...who are we to judge?

We often take other people's advice because doing so seems easier than thinking for ourselves – and, if it doesn't work out, we can blame someone else, right? Nope. The final decision about which path to take was, and always is, yours. Lawyers and financial advisors provide guidance, but you sign the documents they prepare knowing that it's your name on the line. They move on and advise someone else, and your outcome has little effect on them. Your friends and family may be more emotionally invested in how their advice plays out, but make no mistake, the outcome is yours to navigate and the burden is yours to carry.

Section Three Questions

1. **What are some of the ways in which you represent your spouse?**

2. **How do you honestly feel about public displays of affection?**

3. **How do you and your spouse handle social media in your marriage?**

4. **Are you influenced by the court of public opinion? Why?**

Notes

"When we were asked to this, we admit, it took us a minute to figure out what we wanted to say and how we wanted to say it. We looked up the definition of permanent and talked about it, argued a little, wrote something and then erased it. After more debates, laughter and yes, more arguing we finally came up with how we wanted to convey our message. Here is a list of how we feel marriage is permanent for us.

We hope that something on our list resonates with you and inspires your marriage. God Bless!" - Alonzo & Courtney Fulton

Alonzo	Courtney
1. The sum of us is greater than our parts. **2.** We have a God given purpose to fulfill together. **3.** Together, we can overcome any obstacle. **4.** My wife protects me, keeps me safe and covers me when I am vulnerable. **5.** Nobody loves me the way she does.	**1.** He accepts me for who I am, flaws and all. **2.** Simply put, I want no one else. **3.** We've created a perfect family. **4.** He is my peace. **5.** He's seen me at my worst and loved and accepted me.

What the Bible Says

The fourth and *final-P* is reserved for the permanency of marriage. On the previous page *Alonzo & Courtney* provide us with a personal illustration of how they define permanency in their marriage. As you read through the chart they created, you can tell just how personal it became to them as they thought through (and fought through) their statements. We also felt that this "final P" needed to be prioritized, and consequently, we decided to add a fifth chapter to this section. No matter what secular society says, or how the world may define marriage, it is important for those of us who profess our faith in Christ, to know exactly what the Bible says about the permanency of marriage.

Webster's dictionary defines permanent as; *1. lasting or intended to last or remain unchanged indefinitely*. Unfortunately, we live in a society today that has little regard for the honor and sanctity of marriage as God designed it. Cohabitation, "living together," is a common social practice of today. With many in society this immoral practice has gained acceptance and approval. Divorce statistics, although stabilizing, are very alarming. An estimated 2.33 million couples married during 2010. In this same year, an estimated 1.2 million marriages ended in divorce. This statistical data, projected, indicates that one in every two marriages will end in divorce (Universal Almanac, 2012). These tragic statistics are evidence that God's first institution - the home - is in danger and must be patterned after His instructions or the tragedy will be even more catastrophic.

One of the familiar verses in the Bible is Matthew 19:6. This passage contains the words of Jesus in regard to marriage. "*What therefore God has joined together, let no man separate*." This divine principle needs to be applied to the crumbling standards of the marital realm. The apostle Paul reminds us in Ephesians 5:31-33 of the intended purpose of the sacred marriage union:

"For this cause shall a man leave his father and mother, and shall cleave to his wife, and the two shall be become one flesh. This mystery is great: but I am speaking concerning Christ and the church. Nevertheless, let each individual among you also love his own wife even as himself; and let the wife see to it that she respect her husband."

Notice how Paul contrasted the nature and responsibilities of marriage back to the marriage of Adam and Eve (Gen. 2:18-24) to substantiate what has always been true from the beginning. God created for Adam what was needed for his marriage: one wife for the rest of his life. This monogamous relationship is not having one husband or one wife at a time. The principle of monogamy is one man for one woman for life. Marriage is a permanent bond between a man and woman and is intended to last until death (Romans 7:1-3)

Don't Forget to Remember

When it comes to your marriage it is too easy to become lost in the shuffle of life's routine. You can easily forget why you married your spouse, as well as the goals you are working towards. You can also forget the covenants you made as you get caught up in the day to day rush of your life. It is important to take a little bit of time each day to remind yourself of these things. One way that you can do this is by spending time together as a couple. It is important to have a little bit of down time with your spouse each and every day.

If your spouse travels frequently for work, a telephone conversation may suffice. You can also instant-message or text each other throughout the day. This helps to keep your relationship in the present. It is also important to remember the reason and purpose behind marriage. It can become difficult as you deal with your children and all that involves caring for a family to remember what the primary goal of that family is.

You need to take time as a couple on regular basis to make sure that your marriage and your family is pointed in the right direction. Take time to build up the spiritual side of your relationship. Temple attendance, scripture study and couple prayer are things that you can do to help each other stay strong in the gospel. If you are struggling in this area you may want to talk to the bishop about how to work on the spiritual aspect of your marriage. Another important thing to do is to take time every few years (or more often) to spend at least a weekend together as a couple. This time together will give you a chance to get reacquainted. It is important to remember that the foundation of your family is your marriage. As you strive to improve your marriage, the overall spirit in your home will improve as well.

#1: Marriage is not all about you. It's not about your happiness and self-fulfillment. It's not about getting your needs met. It's about going through life together and serving God together and serving each other. It's about establishing a family. It's about committing your lives to each other even though you may be very different in 10, 20, or 40 years from the people you are now.

#2: You are about to learn a painful lesson—you are both very selfish people. This may be difficult to comprehend during the happy and hazy days of courtship, but it's true, and it shocks many couples during their first years of marriage. It's important to know this revelation of selfishness is coming, because then you can make adjustments for it, and you will be a lot better off.

#3: The person you love the most is also the person who can hurt you the deepest. That's the risk and pain of marriage. And the beauty of marriage is working through your hurt and pain and resolving your conflicts and solving your problems.

#4: You can't make it work on your own. It's obvious that marriage is difficult, just look at how many couples today end in divorce. This is why it's so critical to center your lives and your marriage on the God who created marriage. To make your marriage last for a lifetime, you need to rely on God for the power and love and strength and wisdom and endurance you need.

#5: Never stop enjoying each other. Always remember that marriage is an incredible gift to be enjoyed. Ecclesiastes 9:9 says, *"Enjoy life with the woman whom you love all the days of your fleeting life which He has given to you under the sun; for this is your reward in life and in your toil in which you have labored under the sun."*

Enjoy the little things of life with your spouse: the food you enjoy together at home or in restaurants…the movies you like…the little inside jokes nobody else understands except for you…the times you make each other laugh… and the games you play together. Take every opportunity to remind your spouse how important they are to you and how much you appreciate them.

When a husband sends flowers to his wife's job on their anniversary, it's not just about the flowers and the special delivery. When a wife goes downstairs to make her husband's lunch and then leaves a card on the kitchen countertop that reads "Happy Anniversary" it's not just about the sandwich and the care that went into the preparation. Both of these examples are about letting the other person know that they are appreciated and that they remember the reason why they are so special to them.

Now is the time to focus on making memories together, because tomorrow is not promised. Cherish every moment as if it was your last. Plan special dates and weekend getaways. Make sure you reserve time for each other after you have kids. When you both are old, you won't look back and remember the flat-screen television, the cars, money and material possessions you accumulated. More than likely, you are going to remember the things you did together, saw together, and more importantly, the special memories you created together that will last a lifetime.

Making Time

vs.

Taking Time

We know that some of you are scratching your head as you read this sub-title. What on Earth do they mean by Making Time and Taking Time? Well, let us take a moment to explain. When married couples "Make Time" they are intentional about planning the time they spend with one another. It ultimately comes down to prioritizing your spouse and your relationship. In contrast, married couples who "Take Time" do so at the expense of their spouse. Is this a bad thing? Not necessarily, however, it is something that could become problematic over time.

Consider if you will the following scenario:

"A wife comes home after a long day at work. She is both physically tired and emotionally drained. Her husband, who also works full-time, made it home before she did. He cooked dinner for the kids, cleaned up the kitchen, checked their homework, and made sure they took their showers before heading to bed. The wife

expresses her appreciation for her husband taking care of the kids and addressing the needs of the home prior to her getting home. After eating dinner, and detoxing for a half hour, all she wants to do is check on the kids, take a shower, and then go straight to bed. Well, her husband has other ideas about how the night is going to end. He hasn't seen his wife all day and he wants to have some "intimate" time alone with her before they go to sleep. After all, he did take care of the house and the kids before she got home, so in his mind, this should be his reward for a job well done. Unfortunately, his wife expresses just how tired she is and that she is not in the mood for extra-curricular activities".

There are three ways that this scenario will usually play out.

1. The couple agrees to *make time* for each other on another day. This establishes accountability toward one another and a greater appreciation due to the consideration that was shown.
2. The wife gives in to her husband out of guilt or pressure from him. Time is taken from her and it causes her to feel like there was a lack of consideration for her needs.
3. The wife denies the husband and offers no other alternative time for them to come together. This leaves the husband feeling neglected, which leads to resentment.

Couples must also be mindful about how they prioritize their spouse and how they prioritize the other people and things in their life that seek their undivided attention. Nothing makes a spouse "feel some kind of way" than to see that their beloved is showering someone or something else with the attention that was once exclusively shown toward them. Wives, if you are deeply involved in a church ministry and you spend more time at meetings and functions, while neglecting your husband at home…you're going to have a problem on your hands.

Husbands, if you are spending more and more time at work without finding time to call, text or make time during the day to reach out to your wife…you're definitely going to have a problem on your hands. In all things, it is imperative that we learn the art of finding a balance in our lives and in our marriages. If not, the spouse who is feeling neglected will begin to act out in ways that will force you to recognize them, because essentially, they are crying out for your attention. Whenever you neglect *making time* for your spouse, you leave room for the enemy to start *taking time* away from your marriage. Time is precious, and it is the one thing that you cannot get back. As one thing is prioritized, always remember that something else is being neglected. That will preach right there!

Our advice is that you both try to be intentional about making time for one another. The truth of the matter is, making time means making an effort. Sometimes it is a sacrifice. Whether it is planning a mini-vacation, a romantic dinner, a night of intimacy, or quite time alone where you both can talk about issues that are on your heart, try to find optimum time that suits you both.

Based on the plan you come up with, you can then make additional arrangements, so that your common time now becomes a reality. Spending one-on-one time with your spouse is very important when it comes to keeping your relationship healthy, vibrant and alive. Even when it comes to having difficult conversations, we must understand the difference between making time and taking time. Sometimes our emotions can get the better of us and we try to impose our will upon our spouse. We want to *take time* right here and right now to talk about what is bothering us, without even considering if it is a good time to talk them.

Forcing your spouse to *take time* to talk to you about an issue when they are not ready will only complicate matters. They will hear you talking but they will pay no attention to what you are actually saying. This is called being "tuned-out".

Instead, try asking your spouse if they wouldn't mind *making time* in the near future to discuss the issue. This way, both of you have it on your radar, and consequently, you both will have the necessary time to process your thoughts and consider what you are going to say once the conversation takes place.

Embracing Forgiveness

What causes bitterness?

In every marriage, a husband or wife does something that hurts the other. It's bound to happen because none of us is perfect. And in some cases, a spouse has a habit of doing the same thing over and over again, even after the behavior is confronted. Bitterness comes when you hold onto hurt and refuse to forgive the person who hurt you. Most of the time, this comes as a result of ongoing actions of a small nature—lack of understanding, misuse of finances, harsh comments—that build up over time. Each offense takes residence in the heart, and at some point there is no more room left. That's when bitterness is manifested and causes the most damage.

What's wrong with bitterness?

A hardened heart can cause a lot of pain. Here are three reasons why bitterness should be removed from your heart as soon as possible:

1. Bitterness harbors unforgiveness. You may feel justified in your anger. You may think that your spouse doesn't deserve your forgiveness until he or she straightens out. But have you forgotten the mercy that Jesus had for you?

Romans 5:8 tells us that Christ died for us while we were yet sinners. By God's grace, He didn't wait for us to *"get our acts together"* before He provided a way for forgiveness. He gave it to us freely even when we didn't deserve it. At Golgotha as the soldiers gambled for Jesus' clothing, the dying innocent Christ prayed, "Father, forgive them, for they know not what they do." (Luke 23:34). If forgiveness is given freely to us, how much more should we give it to our spouses?

Not only should you desire forgiveness simply because it was given so freely to you, but also, the Bible tells us that there are consequences for unforgiveness. Jesus said, *"If you forgive others for their transgressions, your heavenly Father will also forgive you. But if you do not forgive others, then your Father will not forgive your transgressions"* (Matthew 6:14-15). Seek forgiveness not only for the sake of your spouse, but also for yourself.

Sometimes you will find that your disappointment in a friend can quickly start turning into its own form of bitterness. This is why it is important to seek the Scriptures for guidance. Allow the Word of God to shine brilliant light on your own darkness. There will be certain scriptures that practically leap off the page and speak directly to you about what you're feeling. Consider the following, *"For judgment is without mercy to one who has shown no mercy. Mercy triumphs over judgment."* (James 2:13). I wonder how many hurting marriages would be healed if Christian husbands and wives learned to love mercy as much as they love justice?

2. Bitterness doesn't give your spouse a chance to repent. If you've been holding in your hurt, your spouse may not even know he or she has offended you. Bitterness often comes from hurt that has been suppressed without communication, like filling up a bottle with pressure—eventually that bottle will explode. In the same way, the outburst in your heart can result in a broken marriage, and your spouse never even saw it coming. In this case, go ahead and tell him or her what's been bothering you. Sit down and try to work it out.

Perhaps your spouse does know of your unhappiness, but chooses to continue in the same patterns. This does not negate your responsibility to remove the bitterness from your heart. You still need to give your spouse the chance to repent, although stronger measures, such as marriage counseling, may need to take place.

You may ask, *"How many times does my spouse have to do something before I'm justified in my bitterness?"* Peter had a similar question in Matthew 18:21. He asked, *"Lord, how often will my brother sin against me, and I forgive him? Up to seven times?"*

Jesus replied in verse 22, *"I do not say to you, up to seven times, but up to seventy times seven."*

No matter how many times your spouse may do something, you are still responsible for forgiving him or her.

(Note: If your spouse is physically abusing you, get out of your house and do not stay there. A person who is physically abusive needs extensive counseling and rehabilitation. However, no matter how the situation ends, you can still work on forgiveness from the heart.)

3. Bitterness spreads. Have you ever seen a piece of moldy bread? It appears that there is only one ruined area, but if you were to look at the bread through a microscope, you would see long roots spreading throughout the slice. What appears on the surface doesn't reflect what's really happening below.

Bitterness grows the same way. One little bit of bitterness can start to spread throughout your heart and contaminate your whole body. It will start to manifest itself in your attitude, demeanor, and even your health.

In addition, the spreading can also affect your children and your family. Have you ever noticed how one person's criticism makes everyone else critical, too? It's the same with bitterness. Paul compares it to yeast when he writes, *"A little leaven, leavens the whole lump"* (Galatians 5:6). When you allow bitterness into your life, it extends to your family, your church body, and everyone else involved in your life.

Getting rid of bitterness

You may feel like there is little hope left for your marriage relationship. You may be so full of bitterness that you've convinced yourself that your marriage could never be healed, but let me assure you that the healing begins with yourself. With God, all things are possible (Matthew 19:26).

Here are four steps to take to begin healing from bitterness:

1. Confess your bitterness as a sin. It's so easy to justify our attitude when we've been hurt, but the Bible teaches that bitterness is a sin. Hebrews 12:14-15 says, "Strive for peace with everyone, and for the holiness without which no one will see the Lord. See to it that no one fails to obtain the grace of God; that no 'root of bitterness' springs up and causes trouble, and by it many become defiled..." You must seek peace with your spouse and the grace to forgive.

2. Ask for God's strength to forgive your spouse and diligently seek that forgiveness. In Ephesians 4:31-32, Paul exhorts us to "Let all bitterness and wrath and anger and clamor and slander be put away from you, along with all malice. Be kind to one another, tenderhearted, forgiving one another, as God in Christ forgave you."

3. Make a list of your hurts and find a time to talk to your spouse about it. After you've made your list, pray about which things you can let go and which need to be resolved. If you can let them go, then do so. You may want to physically scratch off each one that you can forgive as an act of faith. Then for those transgressions that are left, ask God to give you the strength to talk to your spouse about them.

Before talking to your spouse, let him or her know that you plan to set aside some undistracted time for you to talk about some issues. As you talk, keep the discussion productive. Start by confessing your own sins to your spouse. Then talk about your hurts. Don't just dump all your irritations and criticisms on your spouse, but speak in love, rationally and gently.

4. Worry about changing yourself, not your spouse. You cannot change your spouse—only God can. But what you can do is allow God to change your heart. Remember, you have also made choices in this relationship that have hurt your spouse and need to be mended. Even though your spouse's sin goes unresolved for now, he or she will answer for it one day before

God (Matthew 10:26). In the same way, God will hold you responsible for the bitterness in your heart. Even though your spouse's sin goes unresolved for now, he or she will answer for it one day before God (Matthew 10:26). In the same way, God will hold you responsible for the bitterness in your heart.

Releasing the Hurt

Have you ever experience a level of hurt that seemed like the worst pain you have ever felt in your life? Whether it was the infidelity of a spouse, the betrayal of a best friend, or uncovering a lie that someone told you, learning how to forgive is not an easy process. However, in order to be set free of the toxic thoughts that infiltrate our minds, we must embrace the simple truth that God requires us to forgive others. Not just with lip-service either. We are talking about genuine, authentic forgiveness. No matter how much we may think or say that we are over the person who hurt us, God has a way of looking right through our masks in order to see directly into our hearts.

Although there is no statute of limitations for dealing with your hurt, there does come a time when the Holy Spirit will make it painfully clear that you need to let it go. Harboring resentment against the person who hurt you is like trying to hold them hostage in your mental prison. Some people hold onto bitterness and resentment because it gives them a sense of empowerment toward the person who hurt them, but at the end of the day they end up tormenting themselves. Unfortunately they only end up incarcerated within the prison walls of their own bitterness.

We need to understand that once we embrace God's forgiveness for ourselves, it will become that much easier for us to forgive others. The gospel of St. Luke 6:37, provides us with a simple remedy, *"Forgive and ye shall be forgiven."* Most people have at least one person in their life that they either find hard to forgive or harbor anger against for one reason or another.

For some the anger is due to a serious hurt, whether physical or emotional, such as an assault, an abusive relationship, or a bitter divorce. For others the anger stems from less important issues, but the anger is just as real and just as debilitating. If this is something that you struggle with, please understand that we are not trying to trivialize or minimize your pain. As you read this chapter, it is our hope that you will embark on a journey of forgiveness that will set you free from the hurt and pain you have experienced. Peter 4:8 says that *"Love covers a multitude of sins"*.

Love and hate cannot dwell together. While we are clear that remembering what happened will always be filed somewhere in our mind, the pain of the incident will eventually leave as long as we allow ourselves to go through the process of forgiveness.

There are many *"Doors of Blessings"* that remain closed to people who are unforgiving, because they don't possess the *"Key of Love"* to open them. Sometimes we have to learn how to get out of our own way! We are not here to judge you if you struggle with forgiving people, but hopefully we can help you see past your pain.

Many of us have hurt people in the past due to our own ignorance, selfishness, and the fact that we simply didn't love ourselves. We all have experienced our share of hurt, but some of us have the uncanny ability to be able to dust ourselves off and move on. On the one hand this can be helpful because it keeps us from dwelling on the hurt and pain of the previous relationship, but on the other hand, it can be harmful because moving on to another relationship (or marriage) too fast is the equivalent of placing a band-aid on an open wound that requires immediate medical attention..

Some of us have been guilty in the past of looking at the person we hurt and wonder why they couldn't seem to get over what happened. We didn't quite understand that for a lot of people, dealing with emotional hurt and pain is a process that requires time. For example, if a husband spends six months lying to his wife about an extramarital affair then he should at least give her six months to process the depth of his betrayal.

Sometimes men can be so insensitive when it comes to how they think women ought to deal with things. That husband that cheated on his wife must take into consideration that just because several months have passed since the affair, and although he may have repented and moved on, it does not negate the fact that it is a fresh, open-wound for his wife. She will need time to process what happened, and it is unfair to place a time-frame on getting over that kind of betrayal.

Consequently, there does come a time where we all have to make a conscious decision to let go of the hurt and pain, and forgive the people who inflicted it upon us. It is at this point that if we willingly decide to hold on to unforgiveness, that we will actually grieve the Holy Spirit and we will not have the grace to receive a healthy healing.

What is a "healthy healing" you ask? It is the type of healing that only God can give. Psalm 147:3 puts it this way: *"He heals the brokenhearted and binds up their wounds."* This means that

God will not only mend your broken heart, but He will take it a step further by caring for your wounds. He loves you that much. Many people try to suppress their pain by avoiding the person who hurt them or by trying to forget that the offence ever happened. This may work for a little while since time does have a way of healing a broken heart, but then there is still the issue of that open wound that needs to be addressed. This explains how someone can have an emotional relapse years later when they finally run into the person who hurt them. It is hard to keep your emotions in check when you are still struggling with forgiveness.

Many people struggle with forgiveness because they think it requires immediate restoration to a manipulative, unrepentant offender. They wrongly assume that forgiveness will mean immediate restoration of trust after it has been deeply violated. Instead we need to understand that forgiving others is more about our peace of mind than it is about our feelings.

Also, you don't always need to track down your offender in order to tell them that they are forgiven, as you may end up disappointed if your forgiveness is not reciprocated. If God desires you to take that approach, He will give you wisdom regarding when, how, and where to do it. That is why we must be clear that forgiveness is first and foremost about God. It is of the utmost importance that we arrive at a healthy place of forgiveness in the context of our relationship with Him. Jesus warned that *"God will not forgive our sins if we do not forgive those who sin against us."* (Matthew 6:14-15). The issue is learning how to transcend the hurt, how to get to a place in your heart and mind where the hurt is no longer holding you back from living a healthy, productive life. A major reason for this is people not being able to forgive themselves. The Bible tells us that *"all have sinned and fallen short of the glory of God."* (Romans 3:23)

When you go to God and confess your sins, the Bible promises that He will not only forgive you but He will cleanse you from all unrighteousness. He is not like man, who will continue to remind of what you did in an effort to keep you bound to your past. You are forgiven and God has forgotten the transgression, as if it never happened. It is time for you to forgive the person or the people who have hurt you. It is time that you forgive yourself for giving them the power to do it, as well as the role you played in it. It is time to look at yourself in the mirror and boldly declare that it is time to move on.

There is no need to keep blaming yourself for what happened by constantly replaying the highlight reel of your past. Instead, you need to take responsibility for getting on with your life and your marriage, in spite of what you have been through or what someone may have done to you. You can do this by shifting your perspective from a victim mentality to a victor mentality.

You can choose now to put the hurt and pain of the past behind you, once and for all, and move forward determined to live the best of the rest of your life. Beloved, God still desires to use you for His glory, and by embracing the power of forgiveness, you will be free to do all that He has called you to do for His Kingdom!

Family Matters

Your life is basically normal…at least most of the time. Your marriage could be better. There have been hard times—maybe even devastating times—but somehow you're working through life. The kids seem happy enough. You provide for them the best you can—a decent education, plenty of outside activities, loving parents. But for some reason, there's a nagging feeling deep inside you, hinting that there's something more. It's as if there is a secret that some of your friends and neighbors know, giving them that special edge on life, but somehow you've missed it.

You've seen the glow from inside the relationships of their homes—even when they're having problems. What makes them different? How can you know the secret? Every couple eventually has to deal with problems in the home—there is no perfect marriage and family. Problems like finances, communication, and conflict resolution are all important to work through in order to cultivate strong, loving relationships.

While on the surface it appears that religion is on the rise, the statistics of divorce, unhappy marriages, and parents having more and more problems with their children are telling a much different story. Even among those who attend church, there seems to be more questions of how to cope with the load of troubles in their life. The bible has a wealth of solutions to many of our questions about what to do every day. We go to church on Sunday and hear a very inspiring sermon. By Monday morning the sermon is forgotten and we go about our business as though we had never heard it. We need to put into practice the lesson from the sermon before we leave the church building. Every day we should read the scriptures used in the sermon on Sunday. Then, every day, we should look for opportunities to live the things we have learned.

Purposeful Parenting

As Christian a parent, your heart's desire is to raise Christian children. It's hard to imagine a son or daughter growing up without Jesus and yet it happens all too often. There are no magic pills to cure this parental concern. What we offer is our experience and thoughts based on what has happened in our own home. Our prayer is that you may find something of value that will help you in your goal to raise Christian children in your home. The points that follow are generic unless otherwise stated. Thankfully there are basic principles that apply to both boys and girls.

Give them quality time - More than anything else, your children need time from you. Viewing television together is a poor substitute for quality time with your children. Going to movies together is not quality time together. You need to be interacting. Quality time involves face time. There needs to be conversation and maybe even some laughter.

Lead by example - You cannot expect your children to read the Bible if you don't read the Bible. You can't expect your children to pray if you don't pray. You can't expect your children to clean if they never see you clean. You can't expect your children to love their neighbor if you don't love your neighbor.

Reassure them they are loved - We have found that the simple yet powerful act of saying "I love you" often can make a huge difference. Verbal reassurance of love is powerful.

Consistently hold them accountable - Children want to know that they have boundaries. They often test those boundaries. When your children cross the line that you have set you must consistently hold them accountable for their choices or they will become confused.

Teach them respect - Teach your children to show respect to adults as early as possible. If they do not learn respect at an early age it is difficult to teach as they grow older.

Share in meaningful conversation - Your children need to know that when they are speaking, you are actually listening. They may not choose the best times to tell you about their day. Often you may be busy or watching a TV program. They need to know that they are more important.

Love your spouse - Your children need to see that their parents are in love. There is nothing so comforting and reassuring as knowing your parents are authentically in love. Boys will learn how to treat women properly, and girls will learn how to bless their future husbands. When Christian parents show their Christian children how to love their spouse, it goes a long way to authenticate their parental teaching.

Blended Families

The Graham's are a blended family of six beautiful children and two adorable grandchildren. While we are not a perfect family, we recognize how God is teaching us how to embrace, support, and love on one another. In a blended family, or step-family, one or both partners have been married before. One or both has lost a spouse through divorce or death, and may have children from the previous marriages. They fall in love and decide to remarry, and in turn, form a new, blended family that includes children from one or both of their first households. That is our story.

Everyone wants "this marriage" to be their last. Not only do they want it to last, but they want it to be healthy and strong. Yet many couples in blended families (also called stepfamilies) know that the odds are stacked against them – very much against them. While the U.S. divorce rate sits around 45 percent, the blended marriage divorce rate is approximately 67 percent (73 percent for third marriages). Apparently, "happily ever after" is a little more difficult to achieve in a blended family.

But the good news is that most remarried couples can beat the odds of divorce and build a successful blended family if they know how to overcome the unique barriers to marital intimacy in a blended family and if they understand stepfamily dynamics. In other words, they can beat the odds of divorce if they "*get smart.*"

Many blended marriages fall prey to divorce because they get blindsided by the pressures and unforeseen dynamics of stepfamily living. Dating couples, for example, naively assume that their first-marriage taught them everything they need to know to have a happy remarriage, and parents who raised their own children assume they know how to be a stepparent. Generally speaking, neither is the case. Another common "blindside" occurs when blended marriage couples, who believe that stepfamilies are just like first-families, discover their step-family is very different from anything they've ever experienced and realize they don't have the tools to successfully manage their home.

Smart blended family couples, however, do a good job of not getting blindsided. They see it coming. They study the qualities of successful blended families, and they work at their marriage. They overcome well-intended but misguided assumptions with "street smarts," and they – and their children – do just fine. Did you ever stop to realize that most of the families of the Old Testament were blended families? Blended families were actually very common in biblical times and are even more so now.

Today in America, approximately 33 percent of all weddings form blended families. Blended families are very common, but being a smart blended family is not. Remember that your children may be dealing with two sets of parents, two sets of rules and two sets of discipline. That is why it is extremely important for a husband and wife to speak the same language. Blended families are a challenge, but we are a living witness that blended-family marriages can thrive when the step-parents keep marriage a priority while being intentional about loving on their children.

Building something that extends far beyond the childrearing years gives your children a foundation to build upon for themselves. Yes, your children are precious and important. Of course, they deserve your love and attention. But make sure you are balancing your care of them with care for your marriage. Try your best to make the transition from one family to another as easy as you can on your children. They should still be expected to obey, but try to understand their frustration when dealing with all the new changes in leadership.

That is why it is important to start laying a good foundation before the marriage. "*Except the Lord build the house they labor in vain that build it.*" (Psalm 127:1) Ask the Lord to give you wisdom in dealing with the challenge of raising a blended family. Work to build a good relationship with your spouse and their children. Don't be afraid to ask God to give you both the wisdom and grace to invest in your marriage, as well as your blended family.

Built to Last

The key to building a *strong Christian marriage* is to make sure the union remains Christ-centered. Couples whose marital relationships are firmly based on a strong belief system are more likely to last. While divorce statistics indicate nearly 50 percent of first-time unions will end in divorce before reaching the ten-year mark, marriages based on biblically-sound principles have greater longevity. Couples who make a conscientious effort to please God and their spouse can weather the storms of life far better than those who exclude spirituality.

Other than a believer's devotion to God, there is no other person more deserving of love than one's husband or wife. The Lord is well pleased when we love the neighbor with whom we share our bed and our life. Consider what the Lord says in the following passage of scripture.

"*And Jesus answered him, The first of all the commandments is, Hear, O Israel; The Lord our God is one Lord: And thou shalt love the Lord thy God with all thy heart, and with all thy soul, and with all thy mind, and with all thy strength: this is the first commandment. And the second is like, namely this, Thou shalt love thy neighbor as thyself. There is none other commandment greater than these"* (Mark 12:29-31).

Men and women intent on building a strong Christian marriage must first understand God's purpose for wedlock. A divinely-ordained institution, holy matrimony was originally intended as a means of procreation and pleasure for the male and female. God ordained the act of marrying as a means of joining a godly man and woman in a monogamous union that would produce children *"after His kind."*

The Creator sought to replenish the earth with generations of men who would seek and serve Him without sin. But because of one man's transgression, the first Adam, sin was introduced to all mankind. Since the Fall of Adam and Eve, male and female have struggled to live harmoniously with increasingly ill-favored results. In the last two decades, the divorce rate amongst Christians and non-Christians has risen sharply, threatening the sanctity of holy wedlock and thwarting the plan of God.

One solution to restore that plan involves born-again believers willing to focus on building a strong Christian marriage by adhering to God's original principles of fidelity and love. In the last days, it will be true believers who can turn the tide of divorce and reestablish the holy ordinance of marriage between godly men and women.

Become the change you want to see

Over the past three years alone we have counseled many married couples who feel sad because they no longer have anything in common with their spouse. We are often asked the question, *"how can I live in harmony with my spouse when we don't see things eye to eye?"* It is common for two married people to grow in different directions, and find themselves not having as much compatibility as they once did. The following two questions are often posed to us.

1. How can you find peace when you and your spouse are not on the same page anymore?
2. Can a marriage work if two people are not like minded, or is divorce the only answer?

We believe the answer to these questions is that it's not easy, but it can be done. The secret to making a marriage work when two people do not seem to have compatibility is found in the following passage of scripture.

"And why worry about a speck in your friend's eye when you have a log in your own? How can you think of saying to someone, 'Let me help you get rid of that speck in your eye,' when you can't see past the log in your own eye? Hypocrite! First get rid of the log in your own eye; then you will see well enough to deal with the speck in your friend's eye." – Matthew 7:3-5

Sometimes just changing your own heart can change the entire marital atmosphere. One area you may need to change is to be more understanding and compassionate when it comes to your spouse. Thinking of your spouse's needs before your own is God-honoring and brings a lot of peace within a relationship. You may need to work on being more accepting of your spouse, which will help you be less critical. Try seeing the good in them in spite of all of the things you currently see.

Now let's be clear here, we are not talking about relationships that are abusive. Those relationships need extra care through professional help. We are talking more about relationships where a husband and wife know the Lord but are on different levels spiritually. This requires both patience and compassion.

Be honest before the Lord and ask Him to shine light on what *you* can do differently to help your marriage. Make sure that your heart is open and that you remain still enough in order to hear His answer. Making this a daily activity will help you to live in obedience to God's Word, and His Word tells us to love sacrificially. We need to love others, including your spouse, as Jesus has loved you (John 13:35). Like we said already, it's not easy. It's not easy to love like Christ loves us. It's not easy to find peace in a marriage that seems incompatible. We certainly cannot do it in our own strength.

That's why it's important to lean on the power of the Holy Spirit. Ask Him to show you to love your spouse, *even though* and *despite* your differences. Commitment within a marriage ought not to be optional, but mandatory. Each day you have to intentionally choose to stay by your spouse, for better or for worse. God is faithful.

He will help you because with His power working in us, He can do much, much more than anything we can ask or imagine (Ephesians 3:20). Living God's way is always the best way. When you allow God to rule in your heart and in your marriage, you will not only honor Him, but you will be blessed by a peace that surpasses all human understanding.

Building a Foundation of Love

Similar to constructing a house, building a strong Christian marriage requires a firm foundation of genuine love. We touched on this a few chapters back when we said that the Greek word for intimate love is "eros," from which the word erotic is derived. But a good marriage is not built on erotic or sexual intimacy alone. The Greeks also term another type of affection as "agape," the unconditional God kind of love. Another kind of love, the affection shared by friends, is called, "phileo."

Couples intent on building a strong Christian marriage must therefore incorporate each type of love: eros, agape, and phileo into the union if it is to succeed. A man and his wife must share a monogamous sexual union, love one another unconditionally, and form a strong bond as the best of friends. A threefold marital bond incorporating each facet of love cannot fail. Over time, eroticism may fail; but affection that is not based solely on sexual attraction can endure.

Husbands and wives who place a high value on developing a lasting friendship may discover that being bosom buddies and chief confidantes can supersede sexual intimacy, especially as couples grow older and may be unable to perform. "*A friend loveth at all times, and a brother is born for adversity*" (Proverbs 17:17). Christians who develop intimate relationships as individuals with the Lord Jesus Christ may be better equipped to share intimacy with a husband or wife. As devoted believers, they will have learned how to seek God, to be led by His Spirit, and to obey His Word.

The process of developing spiritual intimacy is crucial because a husband or wife who is devoted to Christ will likely be devoted to the marriage. The vow to love, cherish, honor, obey, and reverence is taken seriously and becomes a lifelong mantra for those who are submissive to God and to one another. Marital fidelity is a byproduct of building a strong Christian marriage, as couples engage in eros, agape, and phileo love.

When couples love unconditionally, wedlock is not easily broken by poverty or by wealth; sickness or health; or feast or famine. The loss of a job or chronic illness has no lasting adverse effect on husbands and wives determined to make their relationship last. They not only treasure the union; but they also value the relationship forged from two consecrated lives continually governed by the Holy Spirit.

Couples who seek God for guidance and direction in natural, spiritual, emotional and marital matters will find peace, joy, and fulfillment and avoid the pitfalls of discord and divorce. Believers should set aside specific prayer times to come before the presence of the Lord and bring every care to Him, especially in the midst of a family crisis. *"Trust in the LORD with all thine heart; and lean not unto thine own understanding. In all thy ways acknowledge him, and he shall direct thy paths"* (Proverbs 3:5-6).

As Bible-believing couples turn their attention toward building a strong Christian marriage, the outcome can have a positive impact on the viability of the Church-at-large. The world is constantly asking the question, *"What is the significance of the Church?"* The answer, is that it is not a four-walled structure, but it a living organism consisting of a single body of believers from every denomination, socio-economic group, color and creed.

A strong church is built upon strong families; and strong families are made from strong marriages. Our pastor, the

Reverend Dr. Alyn E. Waller, often teaches that if a father is healed, it won't be long before the mother is healed. When the parents are healed then there is a good chance that their children will be healed, and once the family is healed, then ultimately the community is healed.

Christian couples, therefore, have a moral obligation to uphold the sanctity of matrimony and the traditional family unit. By refusing to join the masses who view wedlock as a long-term casual relationship meant to be inevitably broken, we as believers can demonstrate to the world that building a strong Christian marriage that endures is possible with God. It is our prayer that *The 4P's of Marriage* will become a viable resource tool that married couples can use to accomplish this and so much more!

Section Four Questions

1. **Do you believe what the Bible says about marriage?**

2. **What are some things about your spouse you don't want to forget to remember?**

3. **Describe some of the ways in which you can become better at embracing forgiveness.**

4. **Why does family matter to you?**

5. **Do you believe your marriage is built to last? Why?**

Notes

Acknowledgments

There are many people who have participated in *The 4P's of Marriage Workshop,* and who have invested in the development of this project, who we would like to acknowledge. Without them it would have been all but impossible for us to navigate the seasons of our life while attempting to complete the daunting task of completing this book. Their selfless investment of sowing into us over the past two years has given us the confidence, tenacity, fortitude, and freedom to write to our heart's content.

We are indebted to our family, who continually encourage us, pray for us, and love on us. We are truly appreciative of your unwavering love and support. We also would like to thank Reverend Dr. Alyn E. Waller, First Lady Dr. Ellyn-Jo Waller, and the Enon Tabernacle Baptist Church family.

We would also like to extend our deepest gratitude to our children Kristian, Christopher, Nahkyma, David, Drew and Sybrina. Hugs and kisses to our grandchildren Ava and Josiah, as well as our god-daughter Joy.

To our parents, Donald Graham Sr. and Irma Colon-Graham, Connie Graham, Robin and Calvin Scott Bey, our siblings Donny Thomas, Dawn Hayward, Donald Jr., Alex Medina, Arsenio Ray and Elliott Ray, Ayesha Nowell, Nii-Lante' Bailey-Whitaker, and Lacinda Drew.

Thank you to the Hayward, Whitfield and Camp Families, Pastor Byron L. Craig & Evangelist Miriam Craig, and the entire Macedonia Baptist Church Family, Reverend Jerome Glover Sr., Raymond and Victoria Monts, Bishop Eric Wortham and Pastor Sonya Wortham, Reverend Phaedra Blocker, Reverend Maria Lewis, Reverend Blane Newberry, Minister Icie Bagget, Deacon Mike Upshaw, and the entire Enon Fellowship Community. Pastor James Buck and Berean Baptist Church, Pastor Clayton and Belinda Hicks, Seventh Street Baptist Church, Natalie Johnson, April Johnson, Dwight & Deidra Clark-Roussaw and TWOgether Marriages Ministry.

We extend our heartfelt gratitude to Enonge Mallard, Hilary Beard, Darnell Barnes & DSQ Photography, Kimyatta Graham and the Coach/Beckton family, Minister Cheryl "CeCe" Golden, and Kim & John Ebo.

We would also like to acknowledge those married couples who have demonstrated the love, faith, perseverance, and resilience that we often referred to throughout the chapters of this book. They include; Pastor Aaron and Theresa Gray, Rob & Nota Moore, Alonzo & Courtney Fulton, Candace & Hakiem Wilkins, Theo & Kina Small, Elder William & Joyce Taylor, Ramona & Michael Leak, Reverend Leroy & Felicia Miles, Chef Billy & Irene Council Grant, MacDonald & Chenoa Taylor, Martin & Tenita Witherspoon, Nathaniel & Monique Fleming, Nicholas &

Tyree Thompson, Tyrone & Nakia Tate, Curtney & Kendra Lewis, Greg & Valerie Kelley, Terence & Lisa Kadle, Victor & Debbie Fisher, Justin & Dominique Hicks, Tom & Melissa McGlaughlin, Pastor Saleem & Rahisha Wright, and Pastor Tim & Shante Baldwin.

A very special thanks to Kelly Wilwert and *The HUB Community Outreach*, Alpha Nu Omega Inc., *National Alliance on Mental Illness* (NAMI), Rosemont College, Life Coach Institute of Orange County, Inspired Intimacy Radio Show, Caryn & Howard Coff and the entire staff at *Visiting Angels – Jenkintown,* Promise & Destiny Group Inc., Thomas Bailey Associates, and all of the awesome couples who participated in *The 4P's of Marriage Workshop*.

Last but certainly not least, we want to thank our Lord and Savior Jesus Christ who has helped us to navigate the raging waters of life, love, family and marriage. Any wisdom we have shared in this book has been birthed out of the myriad of experiences, good, bad, and indifferent, that God has used to shape our lives for His intended purpose. Lord we love you more than any words we could ever speak, sing, or write. Thank you in advance for blessing this literary work, and it is our prayer that it brings your name the praise, honor and glory that you so righteously deserve!

Scripture References For Husbands

Colossians 3:19 - Husbands, love your wives, and be not bitter against them.

1 Peter 3:7 - Likewise, ye husbands, dwell with them according to knowledge, giving honor unto the wife, as unto the weaker vessel, and as being heirs together of the grace of life; that your prayers be not hindered.

Ephesians 5:25 - Husbands, love your wives, even as Christ also loved the church, and gave himself for it.

Ephesians 5:28 - So ought men to love their wives as their own bodies. He that loveth his wife loveth himself.

1 Timothy 5:8 - But if any provide not for his own, and especially for those of his own house, he hath denied the faith, and is worse than an infidel.

Ecclesiastes 9:9 - Live joyfully with the wife whom thou lovest all the days of the life of thy vanity, which he hath given thee under the sun, all the days of thy vanity: for that is thy portion in this life, and in thy labor which thou takest under the sun.

Ephesians 5:22 - Wives, submit yourselves unto your own husbands, as unto the Lord.

Scripture References For Wives

Genesis 2:18 - And the Lord God said, It is not good that the man should be alone; I will make him a help meet for him.

Ephesians 5:22-33 - Wives, submit yourselves unto your own husbands, as unto the Lord.

1 Peter 3:1-5 - Likewise, ye wives, be in subjection to your own husbands; that, if any obey not the word, they also may without the word be won by the conversation of the wives.

Proverbs 31:11 - The heart of her husband doth safely trust in her, so that he shall have no need of spoil.

Proverbs 31:10 - Who can find a virtuous woman? For her price is far above rubies.

Proverbs 18:22 - He who finds a wife finds a good thing and obtains favor from the Lord.

Proverbs 14:1 - Every wise woman buildeth her house: but the foolish plucketh it down with her hands.

Proverbs 12:4 - A virtuous woman is a crown to her husband: but she that maketh ashamed is as rottenness in his bones.

Proverbs 31:30 - Favour is deceitful, and beauty is vain: but a woman that feareth the Lord, she shall be praised.

Precious D. Graham

About the Author

Precious D. Graham was licensed to preach the gospel in 2010. Born and raised in Philadelphia, PA, she is the co-founder of Promise & Destiny Ministries, and she is also Regional Director of Ministry Affairs of the Keystone region of *Alpha Nu Omega Christian Sorority*.

Precious is a Certified Life Coach and she earned her Master's Degree in Business Administration with a concentration in Project Management from *The University of Phoenix*, and she also holds a Bachelor's Degree in Management and Communications from Rosemont College. Precious has a passion for the kingdom and it is evident in her preaching and teaching. She believes that all are called to be impactful, and she is ready to assist them in reaching their goals.

To learn more about Precious Graham's books, articles, and speaking ministry, or to inquire about having her speak at your next event, please visit her at: www.promisedestinyministries.com

Donald E. Graham Jr.

About the Author

Donald E. Graham Jr. was ordained to preach the gospel in 1997. Born in Brooklyn, New York, he is also an anointed singer and songwriter who has worked with the likes of *Queen Latifah, James Fortune*, and *Ernest Pugh*. Donald is a Certified Life Coach who holds a Master's Degree in Business Management from *Rosemont College* and a Bachelor's Degree in Marketing from Peirce College.

Donald is the founder of Promise & Destiny Ministries, and he is also the author of the Amazon bestseller, *Navigating Your Seasons of Change*, which was named Inspirational Book of the Year for 2013 by *Inspirational Book Review*. In 2015 he released the critically acclaimed book entitled, *Loving Her Means Loving HIM*. He willingly and passionately proclaims the gospel, while using his testimony of faith to help people overcome the mistakes of their past, and realize their potential to live victoriously through Jesus Christ.

To learn more about Minister Graham's books, articles, and speaking ministry or to inquire about having him speak at your next event, please visit him at:
www.promisedestinyministries.com

Established in 2013, *Promise & Destiny Ministries Inc.* was created by Ministers Precious & Donald Graham with the purpose of providing spiritual life coaching, marital enrichment workshops, and literary works that focus on transforming the lives of individuals for the cause of Christ. Through sharing our testimony of faith and the power of prayer, we are committed to helping people fulfill God's *PROMISE* in their lives, so they can walk into their *DESTINY.*

CONTACT INFORMATION

Promise & Destiny Ministries Inc.

(267) 219-5570

promisedestinyministries@gmail.com

Recommended Readings

ISBN 1482541653

ISBN 1482541653

Made in USA - Kendallville, IN
1200033_9781533255440
11.25.2020 0937